Welcome to

Mac
for Beginners

Welcome to Mac for Beginners, the ideal companion to guide you through your first steps with your iMac, Mac Pro or MacBook. In this newly revised edition, we'll explore all the essentials, including basic navigation, shortcuts and back up options. You'll then progress onto discovering all the best OS X apps and features – from Mail to Safari, iTunes to Siri, AirDrop to iCloud. You'll also find all of the latest updates for OS X El Capitan, including handy new Notes features and Split View. We'll also take a look at what to expect from macOS Sierra later this year. You'll learn how to work smarter and get creative on your Mac with programs like Photos, iMovie, GarageBand and Keynote. Finally, we tour the best apps from the Mac App Store, exploring different categories for those with diverse needs and interests. Get started with our step-by-step tutorials and your Apple Mac experience will soon be as smooth as the intuitive system was designed to be.

Mac
for Beginners

Future Publishing Ltd
Richmond House
33 Richmond Hill
Bournemouth
Dorset BH2 6EZ
☎ +44 (0) 1202 586200
Website **www.futureplc.com**

Creative Director **Aaron Asadi**

Editorial Director **Ross Andrews**

Editor In Chief **Jon White**

Production Editor **Jasmin Snook**

Senior Art Editor **Greg Whitaker**

Designer **Perry Wardell-Wicks**

Printed by
William Gibbons, 26 Planetary Road, Willenhall,
West Midlands, WV13 3XT

Distributed in the UK, Eire & the Rest of the World by
Marketforce, 5 Churchill Place, Canary Wharf, London, E14 5HU.
☎ 0203 787 9060 www.marketforce.co.uk

Distributed in Australia by
Gordon & Gotch Australia Pty Ltd, 26 Rodborough Road,
Frenchs Forest, NSW, 2086 Australia
☎ +61 2 9972 8800 www.gordongotch.com.au

Mac for Beginners Fifteenth Edition
© 2016 Future Publishing Limited

 Future is an award-winning international media
group and leading digital business. We reach more
than 57 million international consumers a month
and create world-class content and advertising
solutions for passionate consumers online, on tablet
& smartphone and in print.

Future plc is a public
company quoted
on the London
Stock Exchange
(symbol: FUTR).
www.futureplc.com

Chief executive Zillah Byng-Thorne
Non-executive chairman Peter Allen
Chief financial officer Penny Ladkin-Brand

Tel +44 (0)1225 442 244

Part of the

iCreate™

bookazine series

Contents

Feature
22 Get excited for macOS Sierra

"Explore all the essentials, like basic navigation, shortcuts and back up options"

Feature
8 Read our ultimate guide to your Mac

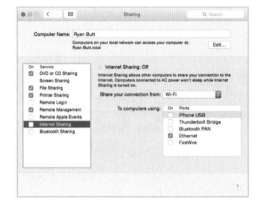

Get started

Understand Apple apps

Feature
128 Create a masterpiece in iMovie

Get creative on your Mac

Work with your Mac

Essential apps

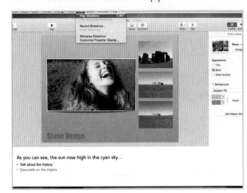

"Macs are great, whether it's work or play you have in mind"

Ultimate guide

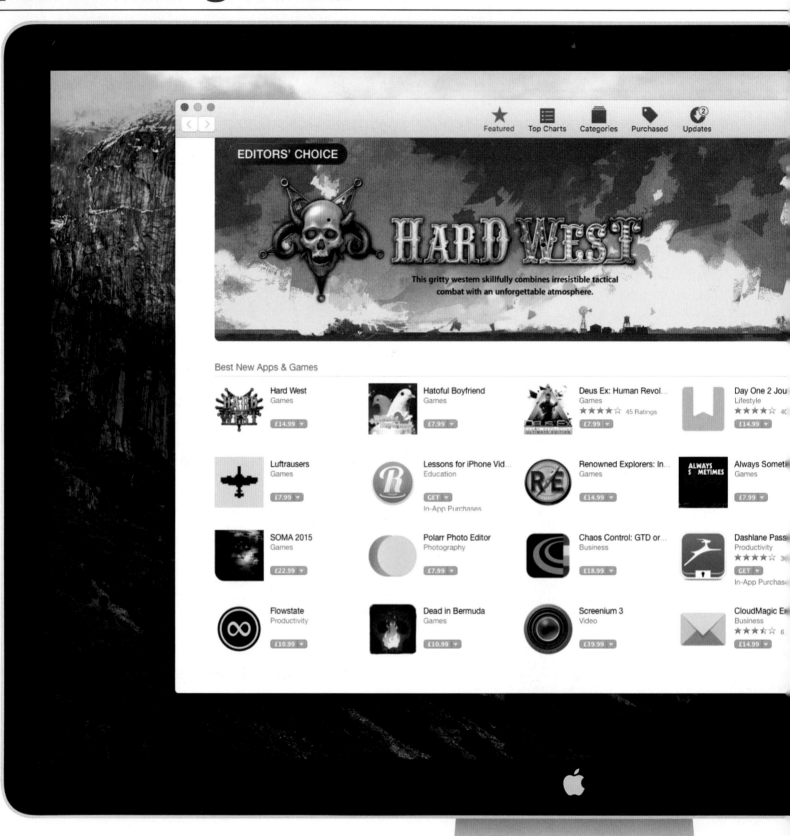

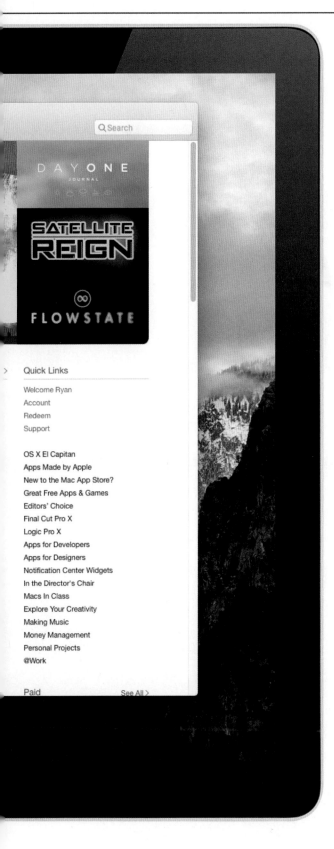

The ultimate guide to your Mac

Taking you through everything you need to know to get started on your Mac

Welcome to the Mac, and welcome to the Mac community. If this is the first time you've owned a Mac, trust us, you're in for a real treat. The Mac is a multi-talented computing phenomenon, part entertainment device, part office workhorse, part creative tool, part media hub. But among all its talents, there's one constant: you'll enjoy using it. If you're used to fighting to get a PC to do the simplest thing, you'll find your new Mac a breath of fresh air. It doesn't get in the way, and the many joys of discovering your Mac's benefits lie ahead.

"Among its talents, there's one constant: you'll enjoy using it"

However easy the Mac is to use – its reputation in this regard is well earned – it's also true that starting out on a new computer or on a new platform can seem daunting at first. Parts of it will inevitably seem unfamiliar. That's where this book comes in. Over these pages we'll take you through everything you need to get going and start enjoying your iMac or MacBook and the latest El Capitan operating system. Soon you'll be taking off with the Mac. It won't be long before you find yourself offering tips you've discovered to other Mac users – and gently extolling the benefits of the Mac to others.

Ultimate guide

Menu bar
All apps (including the Finder) have commands that you can access from this toolbar

View options
Here we're viewing Finder files in Cover Flow mode, though you can show files as lists or icons

Finder
This part shows you your folders, sub-folders and applications and allows you to apply tags to find items more easily

The Dock
This bar contains icons that will launch a variety of handy apps, like Mail

New apps
Mac OS X brings a new iOS feel to your Mac with apps such as Maps and iBooks

OS X

The advantages of the sophisticated Mac operating system

OS X is the operating system (OS) that all Macs use to run their software; the current iteration is OS X El Capitan, but macOS Sierra has been announced as the next release. It is free to download and system updates are regularly available to boost your Mac's performance by going to Software Update in the Apple menu and checking for updates.

OS X has developed over the years to bring a wealth of goodness from iPhone, iPad and iPod touch to the Mac, which complements the features of the previous operating systems perfectly – such as Launchpad, which enables you to see and open your apps in a manner very reminiscent of the

touch-screen iOS dynamics. Since OS X Yosemite, in-built apps include Messages, which lets you send free messages between all Apple devices; Maps to explore the world on your desktop; and Notes, which lets you jot down quick and easy notes that are synced to your iCloud and made available across all of your devices.

Speaking of iCloud, this system now works harder to bind all of your devices together, integrating your emails, calendars, contacts, reminders, documents and more, so that whenever you add, delete or

Date and time
You can view the time as an analogue or digital clock by clicking and holding the mouse button here

Macintosh HD

Cover Flow
You can view folders and their contents as scrollable thumbnails in Cover Flow mode

Background
The desktop wallpaper is set to Wave by default, though you can change this in the System Preferences' Desktop & Screen Saver menu

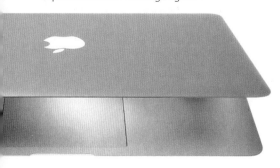

change something on your Mac, these changes also occur automatically on your other devices too. Other features such as the Notification Centre, guarantee you'll never miss an important email or message again.

Entertainment

The Mac has made a name for itself as a creative device, but it'll also help you relax. All your favourite media can be browsed on a Mac, and thanks to the brilliant iTunes, it can all be accessed at the click of an icon.

In the mood to watch a movie or catch the latest episodes of your favourite TV series? iTunes has expanded from its original role as a music player and organiser, and now it can handle your whole video collection just as easily as it does your audio library. What's more, your downloaded videos will be catalogued neatly, organised how you like it so you can easily locate what you want to watch when you want to watch it.

The iTunes Store also holds a growing video collection that you can either rent and watch on your Mac. Both current and classic films are

available, and there's a good choice of television episodes too, particularly when it comes to comedy. You may have a limited time to watch rented media, but it'll be cheaper for it!

Don't forget podcasts either. Some of the video podcasts in the iTunes Store – all free, remember – offer excellent quality.

While you can play videos fullscreen from within iTunes, you can also opt to activate AirPlay – Apple's wireless streaming technology – which lets you stream video as well as audio from your Mac over a Wi-Fi network through Apple TV. So even if you download your videos to a MacBook, iMac or any other Apple device, you can still enjoy them on a really big screen.

Don't forget that you can also watch live or archived television footage on your Mac through a web browser. The BBC's iPlayer (**www.bbc. co.uk/iplayer**) has earned a fine reputation, but several other channels also offer either a live view or an on-demand service of previously broadcasted television shows.

If your entertainment interests are more cerebral, what about reading a book? iBooks is the go-to app in your Dock. The app works in the same way as the iOS version and all of your previous mobile purchases will be synced with your Mac and appear on your iBooks shelf. While reading, an intuitive interface lets you make bookmarks, highlight passages of text and add notes, and the store is just a click away.

Browsing

If we were to make the bold claim that the Mac offers the best way to browse the web, you would probably ask for evidence.

So here's exhibit one: Safari, the Mac's built-in web browser. It's not only one of the fastest and best-looking browsers around, but it also complies with modern web standards, which means that the latest cutting-edge websites should appear exactly as they were intended. Safari also comes with clever features such as private browsing, which hides your browsing history from prying eyes, and a neat 'Top Sites' view that presents small previews of your most-visited sites on one page and lets you visit them with a single click. Very convenient. In Top Sites view, Safari even lets you know when new content has been added to these sites, so you can stay on top of them.

"Browsing the web on a Mac you're far less susceptible to viruses than on a PC"

Another great feature, for those of us who hate the ads that clutter webpages, is Safari's Reader mode. With a single click, webpages are transformed to show the important text in a simple scrolling, image-free window. Safari also comes with many other features, from fullscreen mode to one simple search field for both search terms and web addresses.

Exhibit two: choice. It might surprise many, but Macs come with a far bigger range of web browsers than PCs do. You may not find Microsoft's Internet Explorer here, but on top of other big browsing names (Chrome, Firefox and Opera), there are niche alternatives such as Omnigroup's OmniWeb (**www.omnigroup.com**) for you to try.

Exhibit three: security. You'll be more comfortable browsing the web on a Mac because you're far less susceptible to viruses or other malware than on a PC. Especially as Apple has introduced GateKeeper, a system that provides more control over the apps you download and install and protects your Mac from malicious software. And if it's the kids you're worried about, you can rest assured that Mac OS X comes with a full set of parental controls – found in System Preferences. With the Mavericks update, there are other cool features to enjoy, such as the Sidebar, which provides easy access to your bookmarks, Reading List and shared links from social networks, and a faster all-round performance.

Music

As the creator of the iPod, the most successful music player in history, Apple has long had a special relationship with music. "Why music?" asked Apple legend Steve Jobs rhetorically in 2001, the year iTunes was launched. "We love music. It's part of everyone's life." Nowhere is this view more apparent than within iTunes.

Some will use the app as a simple music player, either with music imported from their CD collection or with that bought directly from the iTunes Store. Through iTunes it is easy to browse and preview single tracks, buy them with a single click and be listening to them on your Mac seconds later. Gone are the days of waiting until the shops are open to get your hands on a much-anticipated release!

Others will use their Mac as an audio hub. iTunes can sync your music library to iPods, iPhones and iPads wirelessly by using your personal iCloud account, so you can take your tracks wherever you go. What's more, with the recent addition of Apple Music, the service has taken a huge market-leading leap. Apple Music is a subscription-based music streaming facility allowing you to access a limitless number of songs and albums for a single monthly payment.

iTunes also comes with a cool feature called AirPlay. If you have a compatible device, such as AirPlay-enabled speakers, an AirPort Express wireless device or an Apple TV, you can stream your music from your Mac straight to them. Home Sharing also allows you to share your music with other iTunes users connected to your home network.

The Mac isn't just great for listening to music. You can create it too, thanks to GarageBand. GarageBand allows you to create your own music, either using the built-in instruments or by recording a real instrument by plugging it into your Mac. Even if you're an absolute beginner, GarageBand can be fun. You can drag pre-built 'loops' of audio onto tracks to build up a song, and even begin to learn how to play an instrument by downloading free basic music lessons from within the program.

Top 10 tips

01: Using Spotlight

OS X's Spotlight search enables you to find text, and image or movie files anywhere on your Mac (even if they're buried deep inside an old email that you were sent ages ago). Click on the Spotlight icon at the top right of the screen and type a phrase into the search field. Then click Show All to see search results from a variety of sources. You can also customise Spotlight to meet your specific needs.

02: Changing brightness/volume

We all like to work in different ways, especially when it comes to sound volume and image brightness. You can control sound volume using sliders within an app like iTunes, or instead drag the master volume slider up or down from the top right of the main menu bar. To change Brightness, simply use the slider in the System Preferences>Displays option.

03: Setting up passwords

If you pop out of the office and leave your Mac unattended, you can get it to lock when the screensaver activates. Go to System Preferences>Security & Privacy and then select the General tab. Click the option to 'Require password after sleep or screensaver begins', then pick a time for this password protection to kick in.

04: Minimising/ maximising windows

The desktop can soon get cluttered with multiple open Finder or app windows. You can use Mission Control to tile them, then click on the one that you want to view full size. Alternatively, click on the yellow Minimize icon at the top left of any window and it'll shrink down to the Dock. The green Maximize icon will make the window expand back up to full size.

Mac OS X is a joy to use compared to Windows, with many user-friendly and powerful features that make your life easier. Here are some top tips to get started with OS X, from changing the appearance of your desktop to creating multiple user accounts and securing your system

05: Change the background

To make yourself feel more at home you can change the default desktop background. Go to Apple>System Preferences>Desktop & Screensaver. Browse through a variety of themed folders for an eye-catching image (or rummage through your Photos Library for something more personal). Click to select a new background.

06: Set up multiple user accounts

To stop others tinkering with your files or settings, give them their own user account. Go to Apple>System Preferences>Users & Groups. Click the padlock and enter your Admin password. Click '+' to add a new account. This user can then choose their own password. Any changes they make to things like the desktop background will be unique to their account.

07: Create and rename folders

To create a new folder, click on the Gear icon at the top of an existing folder and then choose New Folder from the drop-down menu. Alternatively, on the menu bar at the top, head to File>New Folder. By default, each folder is labelled as 'untitled'. Click on the label and then type something more informative.

08: Add applications to your Dock

Docking a favourite application makes it easier to access. Browse to the Applications folder to see a specific application's icon and then drag it to the Dock. You can then launch it by clicking on its docked icon. Remove unwanted docked applications by dragging them from the Dock. They'll vanish in an animated puff of smoke!

09: Save edited files under another name

Let's say you've adjusted the colour of an image using Preview. Go to File>Save As and give the file a name. Click on your house-shaped Home directory and browse to the Pictures folder. Click Save. The edited version of the shot can then be found and reopened by going to the Pictures folder.

10: Log off and shut down

To log off after a hard day's work (or a fun gaming session) go to Apple>Log Out. Click the Log Out button. This will take you to the Mac OS X screen, where you can click Shut Down (or let someone else log in to use their account). Alternatively, press your Mac's power button and choose the Shut Down option.

The Dock

The Dock at the bottom of the screen enables you to access commonly used applications with ease

Finder
Think of this as a doorway to other folders and applications. The Finder helps you find and access any file

Launchpad
Clicking this icon will bring up a window containing all of the apps on your machine, making it easy to launch them

Safari
Fire up Apple's native web browser by clicking here, then enjoy a safe and pop-up-free surf

Messages
The new Messages app lets users send free iMessages to any other Macs, iPhones, iPads and iPod touch devices, including those of your friends

Game Center
Another recent addition to OS X is Game Center, which lets you find games, challenge friends and share scores

Mission Control
Click this icon to view all of your open files and apps, making it easy to find any files or windows currently open on your desktop quickly

Dashboard
Click here to access a variety of handy floating widgets, including a clock, calculator, calendar and even a weather forecast

Mail
Launch the Mail app by clicking here and follow the step-by-step instructions to set up an account

Contacts
This app lets you store vital contact info. With Mavericks you can update this by using all of your Facebook contacts

Calendar
Keep track of important dates and events using this powerful but easy-to-master calendar app

iTunes
Subscribe to Apple Music, browse the iTunes Store and play everything on your Mac. You can also buy iOS apps here

Photos

If the extent of your photo organisation in the past has been to loosely organise them in folders on your PC, or even just to shove prints in a shoebox, you'll be stunned by the organisational prowess of your Mac's Photos app.

Photos gives you a whole new way to easily sort and group your photos. For example, its Faces feature automatically recognises faces in images and lets you add names to them. Photos learns from your choices and can suggest other photos that might include that person. After a while, this automatic recognition gets very good. You can then browse your photos in a special Faces view which gathers all photos of one person together.

In the same way, Photos' Places view uses location information often embedded in a digital image to display their location on a map, while an Events view groups photos by the date that they were taken. And if that's not enough flexibility for you, check out Photos' Smart Folders, whose contents automatically update to hold images depending on the criteria that you set.

If there's a downside to digital photography, it's the tendency for shots to be kept on your computer rather than shared. Photos, however, encourages you to post images to Facebook or photo sharing site Flickr. And if you're after permanent gifts, it can design letterpress cards, books and calendars that can be ordered from within the program.

Storing photos in Photos also makes them available in other iLife and iWork programs, making it easy to add images to slides in Keynote. Photos isn't an all-singing, all-dancing photo editor in the vein of Photoshop, but it will happily handle the basics very well. You can crop, straighten and correct odd colours in a photograph easily and its tool to correct red-eye is almost foolproof.

Perhaps the best feature of all though is that through your personal iCloud, you can activate Photo Stream, which automatically pushes photos taken on your iPhone or iPad to all of your devices, including your Mac, without the need to plug anything in or manually transfer files. Never be without your treasured shots again!

App Store
This bustling online store is where you can purchase apps for your Mac. The format makes it easy to search and browse through apps by category

Reminders
Create quick and easy to-do lists, set yourself alerts and then get them synced across all of your OS/iOS devices

Notes
The new Notes app lets you create quick and easy notes, place them on your desktop and then sync them across all devices using iCloud

Maps
Another welcome OS X addition, the Maps app lets you explore the world in fullscreen and marvel at the wonder of awesome 3D Flyover mode

iBooks
A recent addition to the operating system iBooks lets you access all of your iOS books and read them easily

Photo Booth
The Mac is also a great place to have fun and this photo manipulation app is a big hit with the kids

Photos
This app enables you to store and edit your photos. It neatly organises them by date and time and allows you to create and share albums

Time Machine
If you plug an external hard drive into your Mac, you can then use this app to back up the entire contents of your computer

System Preferences
You can do a host of things here, from changing the desktop wallpaper to modifying the size, shape and location of the Dock

Trash
Click on this icon to have a quick check of its contents, then Control-click on it to find the Empty Trash option

Video

What do *True Grit* and *The Social Network* have in common? Apart from being two box-office blockbusters, both movies were edited on a Mac using Mac-only software. It's a growing trend, and one that's becoming accessible to more people – not just professional film-makers. Ten years ago, you would have needed to sell your house and car to be able to afford that sort of editing functionality, but now you can do it using equipment costing just a few hundred pounds.

If you've got a video camera and a Mac, you already have all the hardware you need. If your camera is a relatively recent model, it's a decent bet that you'll be able to start working with it without even having to install drivers or tweak settings.

While many top-of-the-range movies are edited using the high-end Final Cut Pro on the Mac, iLife's own bundled iMovie is the gold standard of home video editing. Editing in iMovie is as simple as importing your footage and then placing it into a project area. Simply drag and drop to add transitions between scenes or titles, and there's a full array of sound effects that you can use to enhance the audio quality. Even if your original footage isn't top quality, iMovie can improve it. It has a stabilisation tool to correct shaky video and individual clips can be colour-corrected. The

professional look is enhanced through iMovie 11's templates that help you quickly create short and memorable trailers for your work.

The real beauty of iLife applications is the way that they work together. With the iLife media browser, you can add a soundtrack from iTunes or images from Photos or even export your video to iDVD to create permanent keepsakes on disc. That's not the only export option either: you can also share directly to popular video-sharing sites such as YouTube or Vimeo.

And naturally, there's an easy transition to even more powerful tools. Final Cut Pro X isn't too expensive (£199.99/$299.99), and it is the latest version of the famous Final Cut editing suite. It imports existing iMovie projects while allowing you to work with multiple audio and video tracks.

Gaming

It used to be said that the Mac lagged behind Windows when it came to games, but that's far less true now. There are plenty of reasons for this change. The attention of games developers has been grabbed by the Mac's ever-increasing market share. Also, the Mac's transition to running on Intel processors a few years ago resulted in both performance improvements and easier porting of games from the PC platform.

The arrival of the Mac App Store has also proved critical. It has given exposure to Mac games developers who would otherwise struggle for the limelight. That has benefited the developers of games like *Call Of Duty* and *Batman: Arkham Asylum*, which have been some of the App Store's biggest sellers since it launched in January 2011.

The arrival of the Mac App Store has also encouraged existing iPhone and iPod games developers, already familiar with the App Store format and Apple's development tools, to try their hand at the Mac games.

The conversion process is comparatively simple, and as a result, titles that originally grabbed attention on the iPhone, such as *Angry Birds*, *Flight Control* and *Plants Vs Zombies,* have been ported successfully to the Mac. Crucially, in many cases, this transfer has come ahead of their arrival on PC or console systems.

And Mac users don't just have a better choice of games now. The arrival of Game Center means it has never been easier to shop for Mac games (via Game Center's internal link to the Games section of the App Store), and you can also use it to compare scores and challenge your friends online.

There's another reason for the Mac's growth: the arrival on the Mac platform of Steam, a digital distribution platform that boasted 25 million user accounts before it arrived on the Mac. However, now Mac gamers have feature parity: Steam games release simultaneously on Windows and Mac. If you're a Windows Steam user, though, there's great news: if you already own the PC version of a game on Steam, you get Mac versions at no extra charge.

Shortcut tips

The brilliant thing about OS X is the way it lets you control the way your Mac behaves with a few taps on the keyboard. These keyboard shortcuts can speed up the way you interact with your Mac, so you are able to clear away clutter, find files fast or jump between open applications in a click. By knowing the keyboard shortcut for a command, you no longer have to drag the mouse up to the main menu and rummage around in submenus!

We'll cover shortcuts that work with OS X, plus show you some generic key combinations that will work in most applications (like copying and pasting). Many shortcuts use the key with the Apple logo on it – we'll refer to this as the Command key in our tips, since some wireless keyboards don't feature the Apple logo on the Command key. The key with Alt on it is the Option key.

Command+Z
This is the Undo function in most applications.

Option+Shift+Command+Escape
If you hold these keys down for three seconds, you'll Force Quit the currently-open app. Only do this if an app freezes up.

Command+C
Copies selected text, documents or even images.

Command+Shift+3
Takes a screenshot of your display and saves it as an image file to the desktop.

Command+V
Pastes anything you copied with the Cmd+C shortcut.

Command+S
This shortcut saves the current document, using the same name.

Command+N
This will give you a new document in any application you're using.

Command+Tab
This activates a handy mini-Dock. Keep pressing Tab to switch between currently open applications.

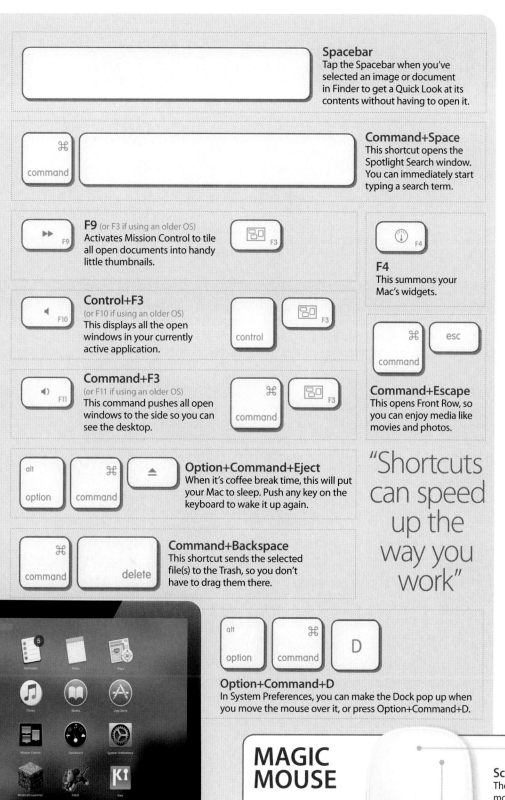

Spacebar
Tap the Spacebar when you've selected an image or document in Finder to get a Quick Look at its contents without having to open it.

Command+Space
This shortcut opens the Spotlight Search window. You can immediately start typing a search term.

F9 (or F3 if using an older OS)
Activates Mission Control to tile all open documents into handy little thumbnails.

F4
This summons your Mac's widgets.

Control+F3
(or F10 if using an older OS)
This displays all the open windows in your currently active application.

Command+F3
(or F11 if using an older OS)
This command pushes all open windows to the side so you can see the desktop.

Command+Escape
This opens Front Row, so you can enjoy media like movies and photos.

Option+Command+Eject
When it's coffee break time, this will put your Mac to sleep. Push any key on the keyboard to wake it up again.

Command+Backspace
This shortcut sends the selected file(s) to the Trash, so you don't have to drag them there.

"Shortcuts can speed up the way you work"

Option+Command+D
In System Preferences, you can make the Dock pop up when you move the mouse over it, or press Option+Command+D.

MAGIC MOUSE

Right click
If you do this while selecting a word in Safari, you can choose 'Look Up in Dictionary' from the context-sensitive pop-up menu.

Scroll
There's no wheel on this mouse; just slide your finger down the middle to scroll.

Control+Scroll
This combo enables you to zoom in to get a magnified view of what's on the screen.

Office

If you didn't think of the Mac as an office workhorse, think again. Easy to use, supremely resistant to viruses and coming with a reputation for reliability, Apple desktops and laptops tick plenty of hard-nosed business boxes.

But what about the software? The good news is that the dominant office software is available on the Mac – and it's just as good as the one on Windows. Microsoft Office 11 for Mac has virtually the same functionality as its PC sibling, but looks better. You can swap Word and Excel files with PC users and even share Outlook calendars on a connected server. Plus, recent Macs come with built-in support for Microsoft Exchange Server 2007, so if you use Exchange at work, the chances are that you can access all your emails and calendars at home too.

Apple has been making its own steps into the office space too. Its Mac-only iWork suite, the components of which are now free to download, also features word processing, spreadsheet and presentation capabilities. If its word processing and spreadsheet tools lack the complete range of functions of Microsoft's equivalent tools, they are at least arguably easier to use. iWork's Keynote presentation software is a genuine alternative to PowerPoint, with its more polished templates and more impressive transitions.

iWork files are also Office compatible: files saved in Office on the PC can be opened in Pages, Numbers and Keynote, while you can export them from iWork in PC format too. What's more, you can sync documents to your iCloud and access them from any computer or iOS device in the world to continue working on them – and everything saves automatically so you don't have to worry about work being lost. The only thing missing in both the Microsoft Office and iWork suites is a decent database, but even here you're spoiled for choice: pick between Filemaker (**www.filemaker.com**) or iDatabase (**www.apimac.com/mac/idatabase**), which presents a budget alternative.

Office work isn't all about spreadsheets, letters and slideshows, though. What about managing your accounts? There's plenty of choice here too. AccountEdge (**www. mamut.com/uk/mac/ accountedge**) and Business Accountz (**www. accountz.com**) are both reasonably priced and capable desktop applications. So you see, Macs cover all bases when it comes to personal and professional use.

Productivity

Keeping yourself organised has never been more demanding. But your Mac, and its built-in calendar application, can help you to keep on top of things. Calendar (formerly iCal) supports multiple calendars – so you can track work and family commitments separately – and you can view calendars in several ways: by day, week or month. You can invite others to events you create and set an alarm to remind you before it starts.

The calendar also lets you sync appointments with iPhone, iPod touch or iPad Calendar apps, using iTunes as a handy go-between. If you use Apple's iCloud service, you will also have the ability to sync your calendar without a physical connection, and you will be able to share calendars between multiple Macs too.

Beyond its calendar, the Mac has been built to take control of the chores while you do what you want to do. For example, every computer user knows they ought to back up regularly, but the organising of backup discs and choosing what to copy invariably gets in the way. Not on a Mac. Here, backing up is as simple as attaching an external drive. Apple's Time Machine backup utility takes care of the rest.

To be truly productive, you need to get as much done as possible while avoiding those repetitive tasks that can take up a lot of your time and become quite frustrating. Automator is a drag-and-drop tool for automating common chores. You build a workflow by piecing together actions and the saved result automates the task in the future. With some applications, you can just record your mouse and keyboard movements and save the result to an Automator workflow, where they can be stored and replayed. It's like programming without the hard work.

Another often overlooked productivity treat for many Mac users is Services, which comprises small pieces of functionality that can be shared between different applications. Accessed from the application menu (if you are in iTunes, for example, Services can be found under the iTunes menu), services suitable for the current application automatically appear – so if you're working in a word processor, you might see a service to send the currently selected text in an email. Furthermore, if you don't find a service you would like to see, you can easily build one of your own – using Automator, of course. There are plenty of options on your Mac to make you more productive.

iTunes top tips

Organise your music collection with iTunes, stream over 30 million tracks with Apple Music and sync songs with mobile devices

The way that we manage music has changed dramatically since iTunes and mobile devices like the iPod and iPhone came along. Once you've copied your CDs into your iTunes app, you'll rediscover music you haven't listened to for years. Think of iTunes as your personal digital jukebox! You can use it to store and organise your music collection, as well as discover and buy new music (or movies) via the iTunes Store. That's moved on even more with the addition of Apple Music, with its paid-monthly subscription service and 24-hour radio station, Beats One. Here's are some of the ways you can take advantage of iTunes 12, the latest version.

MacBook

New software

Like other apps, iTunes is always evolving to include improved performance and extra features. You may be informed that newer versions of iTunes are available when you open the app, but you can also check out any updates by going to the iTunes menu (look next to the Apple icon in the top menu bar) and choosing Check For Updates. You can then download and install the latest version of iTunes.

MiniPlayer

To reduce the size of the iTunes interface, simply go to Window>Switch to MiniPlayer. This turns iTunes into a small floating mini player that enables you to perform useful commands like playing, pausing, jumping forward to the next song or even searching your library. You can adjust volume here too by using the slider in the AirPlay menu.

Add to My Music

If you're using the Apple Music trial or you're all officially signed up, you have access to the entire iTunes catalogue, which totals a staggering 30 million tracks. When you come across music that you want to add to your library (you don't have to buy it), find the three-dot icon and select Add to My Music from the drop-down menu that appears. That track or album will now live in the My Music tab in iTunes.

"Once you've copied your CDs into your iTunes app, you may rediscover music you haven't listened to for years"

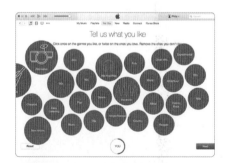

For You

The more you use Apple Music, the better it gets at predicting what you want to hear. If you spend a little time telling the streaming service what you like (head to your user account and select Choose Artists For You), including genres and artists, then your For You tab will be filed with personal playlists guaranteed to make you smile. For You also picks up on every time you 'favourite' a track or album by clicking on the heart symbol. You'll be amazed by how accurate Apple Music soon becomes.

Get Album Artwork

If an album in your Library isn't displaying the cover, right-click on it and choose Get Album Artwork. iTunes will then trawl an online database for appropriate covers. If no album art can be found then you may need to adjust the info. Right-click on the album, choose Get Info and then tweak and amend the info before trying again.

Sync an iPhone or iPad

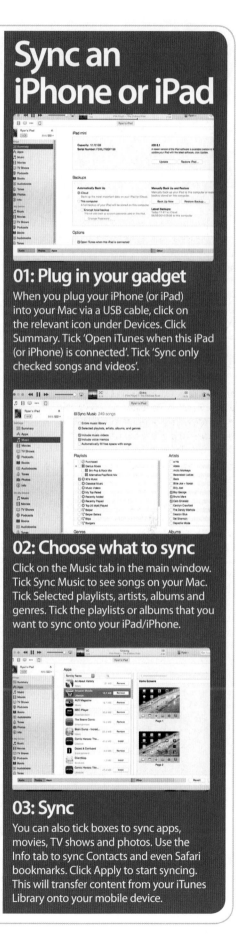

01: Plug in your gadget

When you plug your iPhone (or iPad) into your Mac via a USB cable, click on the relevant icon under Devices. Click Summary. Tick 'Open iTunes when this iPad (or iPhone) is connected'. Tick 'Sync only checked songs and videos'.

02: Choose what to sync

Click on the Music tab in the main window. Tick Sync Music to see songs on your Mac. Tick Selected playlists, artists, albums and genres. Tick the playlists or albums that you want to sync onto your iPad/iPhone.

03: Sync

You can also tick boxes to sync apps, movies, TV shows and photos. Use the Info tab to sync Contacts and even Safari bookmarks. Click Apply to start syncing. This will transfer content from your iTunes Library onto your mobile device.

Mac App Store

Browse thousands of Mac applications, all located in one convenient App Store

Launched back in July 2008, Apple's original App Store was initially accessible via an app on the iPhone – and subsequently the iPod touch and iPad – enabling users of those devices to peruse thousands of downloadable apps designed for iOS devices. Apps span a wide range of categories (from Photography to Education) and let you extend your iPhone's functionality in many exciting ways. The iPhone-centric App Store has proven incredibly successful, so there was little surprise when a Mac OS X App Store appeared early in 2011. On its first day, the new Mac App Store sold a million apps.

The Mac App Store enables you to find useful software for your iMac or MacBook in one convenient place, without having to trawl the internet. To browse it, you'll need the Mac App Store app, which is available by default with OS X Mavericks (you can use your Apple>Software Update menu command to install the latest version of older operating systems). Once you've updated Mac OS X, the Mac App Store will appear in your Dock. Double-click on the app's icon to fire it up.

As there are thousands of Mac apps to explore, finding what you need can be daunting, so it's worth rummaging through one of the 21 categories first. As with the iOS App Store, these Mac app categories cover a wide range topics, including Games and Social Networking. Once you've found a category that you're interested in, you can refine your search by looking at the Top Paid or Top Free Apps to see what is popular. Alternatively, you can search the App Store with a relevant keyword. Once you've clicked on an app that catches your eye, you can find out more about it by viewing screenshots of its interface. More importantly, you can read the reviews of people who've already downloaded the app to see whether it's worth your time (and money!).

Browse
Click here to browse apps by categories. These span from Business to Weather, taking in Music and Photography along the way too

Select
Once you've selected a category, a series of featured apps will appear here. When something takes your fancy, click to go to the app's page for more information

Communication

The Mac is all about communication, whether by email, text message or video. Apple Mail, the email program that sits in the Dock of every Mac, is a superb way to keep in touch with friends, family and colleagues. It can handle multiple email accounts and, thanks to the Mac's Spotlight search engine, all its messages can be

searched in an instant. Want to add files or photos to your email? Just drag them over your message window or use Mail's photo browser to grab snaps from your Photos collection. In Mail, email doesn't need to be drab: you can style it using beautifully designed templates.

Mail is clever too, analysing the contents of incoming messages, not just to check whether they contain spam – in which case they will be neatly removed from view – but also to interpret the contents. So if you get an email asking you to meet someone tomorrow at one, you can click on this invitation to add it to your iCal calendar. And Mail

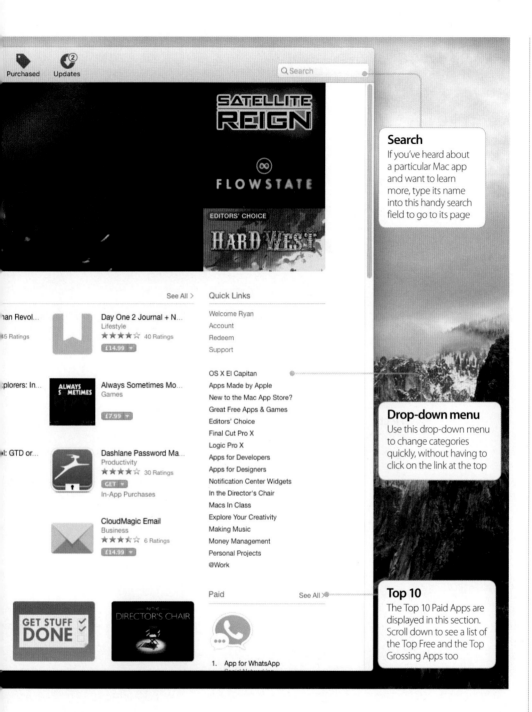

Search
If you've heard about a particular Mac app and want to learn more, type its name into this handy search field to go to its page

Drop-down menu
Use this drop-down menu to change categories quickly, without having to click on the link at the top

Top 10
The Top 10 Paid Apps are displayed in this section. Scroll down to see a list of the Top Free and the Top Grossing Apps too

Creativity

The Mac, at its heart, is a creative tool. It seems to have always been that way. The desktop publishing industry began on the Mac back in the Eighties and, 30 years later, today's web design industry still favours the platform. How can that be? Perhaps the Mac's ease of use has something to do with it, or the fact that creative peripherals, such as drawing tablets, are designed to work seamlessly on it.

It's as likely, though, that the quality of Apple's hardware strikes a note with creatives. And that applies from a practical, as much as an aesthetic, point of view. Those Mac screens – particularly the larger iMac displays – not only look great, but offer great colour reproduction. And the Mac's built-in ColorSync technology ensures that what's great-looking on screen will look just as good (and colour-accurate) when it prints out.

Above all, it's the software that appeals. A quick scan of the Mac App Store will reveal dozens of cool budget drawing and illustration tools – not forgetting Pages' superb layout tools – while the industry-standard design applications all work well on the Mac, from QuarkXPress to Adobe's Creative Suite, which comprises popular applications such as image editor Photoshop, drawing tool Illustrator and page layout application InDesign.

The web is the catalyst for much creative work nowadays. For those who want to put a creative site together without having to get their hands dirty with code, Pages, which comes as part of the iWork suite, is a great start. You can base your website on pre-built templates and customise it by dragging other iLife components – video from iMovie, images from Photos or audio from iTunes – into it. Instead of having to hand-code functionality to add features such as embedded YouTube videos, you can just drag a widget to your page. Publishing to the web is a single click away.

If Pages whets your appetite to get more serious about web development, there are plenty of more powerful tools available to help. Another Mac-only tool, Coda (**www.panic.com/coda**), offers a single window coding environment that's popular with Mac web coders and developers.

works neatly with the Mac's own application for storing contacts – Address Book – which syncs with your iPhone or iPad via iCloud, so your contacts are with you all the time.

Facebook is becoming an ever more popular way to communicate and while most people are happy using the Facebook website, there are plenty of Mac applications that integrate with it. Even Photos offers a way to upload your images directly to your Facebook account – and comments about the photo made by Facebook friends can be seen within Photos. You can also use the web to keep up with your Twitter contacts – although it's easier to

use one of the Mac's own applications: the Twitter application itself is a free download from the Mac App Store.

FaceTime is another cool feature that allows you to have a video chat with other FaceTime users, whether on the Mac, iPhone, iPad or iPod touch. If you prefer to do your talking via text message, then Apple's own Messages app is perfect.

But if you want to keep up with friends using other text messaging services, such as AOL Instant Messenger, look no further than the excellent Adium (**www.adium.im**). The possibilities for communication are endless.

"There are dozens of cool budget drawing and illustration tools in the Mac App Store"

The complete user guide to
macOS

Inside Apple's incredible, all-new operating system for your Mac

Ever since Steve Jobs introduced the Macintosh for the first time in 1984, the dream of being able to talk to your Mac and have it answer back has lived in the minds of Apple fans. With the release of macOS Sierra, that dream has become a real and powerful reality.

When Sierra launched as a free download late in 2016, you could begin using Siri on your Mac. But that wasn't the only exciting prospect for those upgrading, because the recent update is packed with new features, tricks and technology to make your life easier, faster and far more fun.

There are changes from the moment you wake up your Mac from sleep thanks to Auto Unlock, which allows your Apple Watch to automatically log you back in to your user account. Those with multiple Apple devices will also benefit from other great Continuity features, like a Universal Clipboard and cross-device folders that take iCloud Drive to the next level. How many times have you dropped something on your desktop, but then had to send it to your iPhone? Now, thanks to iCloud Drive, the documents on your desktop will be available to you, wherever you are.

And that's just the start. With new Apple Pay features, Optimized Storage technology, Picture-in-Picture video and more, macOS Sierra is shaping up to be an incredible release for Apple.

MacBook Pro

Will my Mac run macOS Sierra?

iMac
As long as your iMac is from late 2009 or later, you can run macOS Sierra – however, older machines may not benefit from all of the newest features

How different is macOS?
OS X has a new name but the system runs on the same core systems. Aside from some small design tweaks it will be familiar to OS X aficionados.

MacBook
The original plastic MacBooks won't run Sierra, but aluminium models from late 2009 or newer will have no problems. Of course, the new Retina MacBooks have it too

Mac Pro and Xserve
The older, silver Mac Pros are upgradeable to Sierra as long as they were produced in 2010 or later. Owners of the new, cylindrical Pro can also get the update

MacBook Pro
The earliest MacBook Pros that run Sierra are those from 2010. Check the age of your Mac by clicking the Apple logo and choosing About This Mac

MacBook Air
MacBook Airs from 2010 or later can upgrade, but older machines may start to see reduced performance due to power-hungry new features

Mac mini
As long as you own a Mac mini that was made since 2010 you can download Sierra, although once again older machines may not get all the new features

What's new in macOS Sierra?

Auto Unlock
If you own an Apple Watch, logging in to your Mac is as simple as moving close to your machine with it on your wrist. It really is that easy!

Siri
Making its debut on the desktop as an integrated system in macOS Sierra, Siri has new specifically designed capabilities.

Apple Pay
Finally, Apple Pay comes to the Mac. When you see the icon, click it and authorise the payment with Touch ID on your iPhone.

Universal Clipboard
Copy and paste works across all of your devices. Copy on your iPhone, paste on your Mac. Simple!

Tabs upgrade
A new system built-in to Sierra allows any app on your Mac to support tabbed browsing, including third-party apps.

Optimized Storage
This cool new feature stores your least-used files in iCloud, and automatically deletes old files you don't need.

In the cloud
iCloud Drive has expanded to include files stored in Documents and on your desktop, so they are then available on every device.

Photos
A new Memories tab collates photographs from holidays and days out using smart algorithms, while Places makes a welcome return.

Picture-in-Picture
Now an available feature on your Mac, make a video 'float' over your other windows so you can keep watching.

Messages
iOS 10 gives Messages a major upgrade, and while the Mac can't do all of the same things, it has still had some awesome new updates.

Siri

Apple's personal assistant debuts on the Mac

Siri has grown up a lot in the last few years. Apple's personal assistant has learnt about sports scores, gained new accents and even allowed activation by voice. And in macOS Sierra, Siri appears on the Mac for the very first time, with some nifty new features on show.

Of course, Siri can still complete all of the same tasks as on your iPhone and iPad, like checking weather, setting alarms and contacting your friends, but there are some new, Mac-specific features that are being added to make working with your Mac easier than ever.

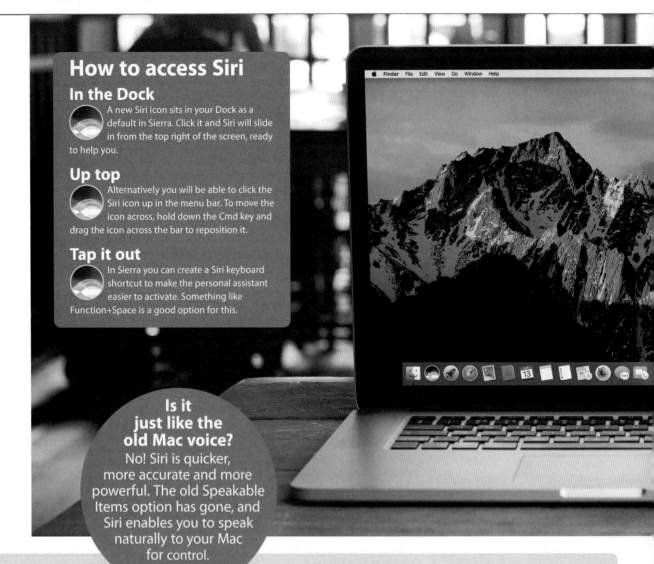

How to access Siri

In the Dock
A new Siri icon sits in your Dock as a default in Sierra. Click it and Siri will slide in from the top right of the screen, ready to help you.

Up top
Alternatively you will be able to click the Siri icon up in the menu bar. To move the icon across, hold down the Cmd key and drag the icon across the bar to reposition it.

Tap it out
In Sierra you can create a Siri keyboard shortcut to make the personal assistant easier to activate. Something like Function+Space is a good option for this.

Is it just like the old Mac voice?
No! Siri is quicker, more accurate and more powerful. The old Speakable Items option has gone, and Siri enables you to speak naturally to your Mac for control.

Siri's Mac-specific commands

Siri works just like on iOS, but there are some special commands for your Mac

Ask for specific files by saying something like "Show me the files I worked on last month about the Development presentation." Siri will find these files and present them to you.

You can even refine a search – so, after that first query, you could say "Just show me the files Phil sent me that I tagged as important." This will filter your search results accordingly.

Siri can search the web, but now you'll have the option to drag and drop image results into a document – just say "Search for pictures of…" and you're good to go.

If you want to check in on your Mac's status, you can do just that with Siri too. Simply ask "How much free space is there on my Mac?" and Siri will present you with an update on your storage situation.

Saying something like "Show me all the images in my Downloads folder" will quickly bring up a list of any image files you've downloaded recently, so you can instantly use them in other apps.

If you want to use Siri more creatively, you can say something like "Show me the photos I took last month" and you'll be able to browse through your shots instantly.

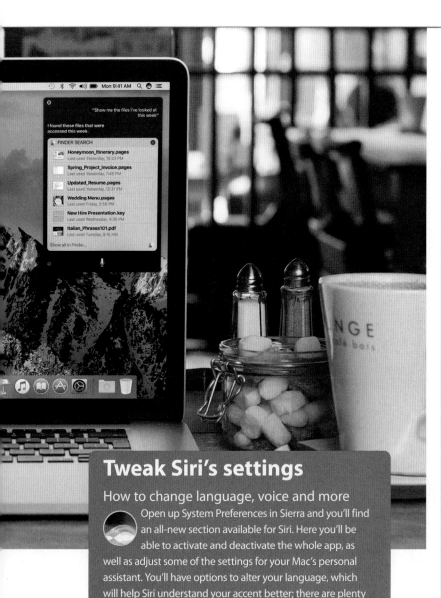

Which Siri searches are you able to pin in the Notification Center?

Did you know that you can pin Siri searches and have them automatically update in your Today menu?

One of Siri's new abilities to appear on the Mac is the option to add results to the Notification Center. In the top right of some Siri search results you'll find a '+' icon. Click this and the window will be added to your Notification Center's Today view, so you can quickly access it.

File searches

If you ask Siri to find a particular file but want to save it for later, click the '+' icon, and when you need the file you can just open Notification Center and drag it over to wherever you need it.

Sports updates

Ask Siri about an upcoming game from your favourite team and you'll see all the details. You can then add this to Notification Center to keep an eye on the score while you work.

Weather

If you want to check the weather in a certain location, just ask Siri and it'll look it up for you. Even better, you can add this search to Notification Center and save it for regular checks.

Tweets

To find the latest tweets about a specific subject or from a certain person, just ask Siri to find them. Save them to Notification Center and you'll be able to check on the updates whenever you want.

Wolfram Alpha results

If you're studying and need to keep checking equations or other facts, get Siri to check them with Wolfram Alpha, then save them to Notification Center so they're there when you need them.

Web searches

Looking for an image is simpler with Siri, and now you can save your results. So even if you don't need the results right away, they're there when you do come to use them later.

Tweak Siri's settings

How to change language, voice and more

 Open up System Preferences in Sierra and you'll find an all-new section available for Siri. Here you'll be able to activate and deactivate the whole app, as well as adjust some of the settings for your Mac's personal assistant. You'll have options to alter your language, which will help Siri understand your accent better; there are plenty of settings, so find the best one for you rather than just leaving it on the default option. You can also adjust the voice Siri uses, choose whether or not Siri gives vocal feedback on every command, alter the microphone input and change the keyboard shortcut used to activate it.

Export Siri content

Drag and drop Siri searches into apps

When you search for something in Siri, you can drag and drop the results from the Siri window into the application you're using. This includes both documents and images on your Mac and results from online searches. Simply ask Siri to find something for you, like "Search for pictures of ice cream cones," and Siri will bring up image search results. From here you can drag any image you like from the Siri window into your document. This works in any app across your system, and can also be used to open files by dragging them into the relevant Dock icon, or add images on your Mac to documents quickly.

Copy & paste between devices

Use Universal Clipboard to copy images, video and text from iPhone to Mac

How many times have you been reading something on your iPhone or iPad, or found a photo online, and wanted to add it into a presentation or document you were working on over on your Mac? Well, with macOS Sierra and iOS 10, you can copy text, images and more from one device, then switch over to the other device and paste it in. It really is as simple as it sounds – no extra menus or messing about with tabs in Safari. Just copy on one device, and paste on the other.

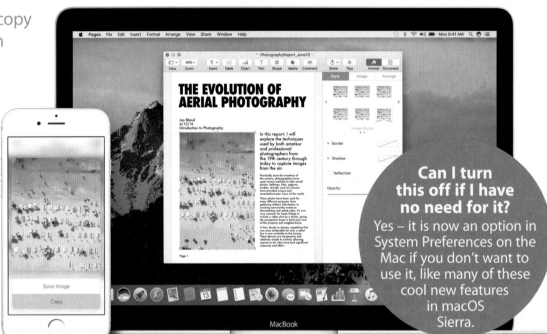

Can I turn this off if I have no need for it?
Yes – it is now an option in System Preferences on the Mac if you don't want to use it, like many of these cool new features in macOS Sierra.

Unlock your Mac with an Apple Watch

Be more secure, but keep things simple

We always advise that people add a password to their Mac for when they step away from their machine, but secure passwords are long, difficult to type and hard to remember. That's why this new feature is so welcome – in macOS Sierra, simply sitting down at your Mac while wearing your Apple Watch unlocks it so you can do what you want instantly.

1 Wear your Watch
You'll need to have your Apple Watch on your wrist, and if you have a passcode you'll need to have entered it so that the Watch knows that you are the one wearing it.

2 Wake your Mac
Walk up to your Mac and either open the lid to wake up the screen, or tap any key (or the mouse) to wake it from sleep and make the lock screen appear, with the passcode prompt on-screen.

3 You're in!
Simply move your Watch close to your Mac, like you were about to type something. Your Mac uses time-of-flight networking to securely confirm that it is you unlocking the device by being that close.

Will my Mac unlock from across the room?
No – you need to be close enough to your Mac that you can use it for it to unlock, so don't worry about others jumping on without you knowing.

Let your Mac save space automatically

Optimized Storage keeps rarely used files in the cloud

 We store loads of stuff on our Mac, whether it's hundreds of thousands of photos, dozens of movies in iTunes or old iOS device backups that we've long forgotten about and no longer need. In macOS Sierra, Apple can help you free up space on your Mac by storing your least-used files in iCloud, and deleting the ones you really don't need any more. Here's how it works.

How effective is this?

Very! Apple turned everything up to maximum and saved 130GB on its example machine. This is obviously an extreme example, but it could still work wonders for your Mac.

Store in iCloud
You can choose how your Mac deals with old files here, by storing old photos and files in iCloud when your Mac starts running low on space, and keeping only the most recently-used files.

Optimize Storage
Things like iBooks that you've read, movies that you've watched and email attachments just take up valuable space, but with a few clicks you can let your Mac clean these up for you.

Scheduled Trash removal
How full is your Trash right now? Ours had 330MB when we just checked. Thankfully, Sierra can automatically delete files

when they've been in there for more than 30 days, saving you a great deal of disk space and the hassle of you periodically doing this yourself.

Reduce clutter
Old files dotted all over your Documents folder can be hard to find and delete. In Sierra, your Mac groups them all for you, so you can quickly sort through and delete those you don't need.

Preview effectiveness
On the left of the window you can take a look at how much space has been saved by using the settings you're currently using. Click each one to see more options.

Access your Mac's desktop anywhere

iCloud Drive is now more powerful and useful than ever before

 iCloud Drive is great – it helps users store important files in the cloud and access them anywhere, on Mac, iPhone and iPad. But when we're working on our Mac, where do we put all of the things we're working on? Often it's our desktops that become the easiest place to drop items, which is why Apple has upgraded iCloud Drive to now include your entire desktop as well as your iCloud Drive folder. Now, when you forget to move that important presentation or document into the right folder, it's not a problem – you can just grab it from your iPhone.

Is it just my desktop that's uploaded?

No, you can choose to upload all the files in your Documents folder if you want, so everything you could ever need will be available.

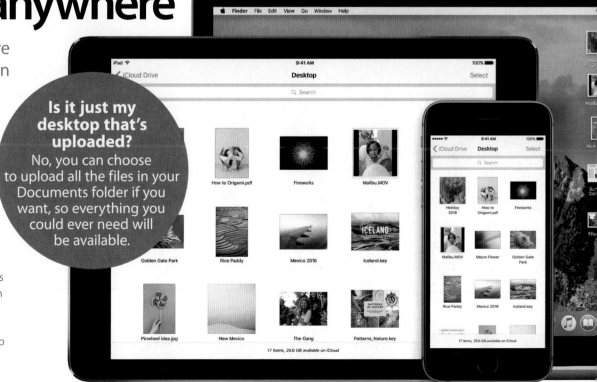

Rediscover memories in Photos

A rundown of what's new in macOS's most popular image editor

Photos had a big upgrade when iOS 10 and macOS Sierra launched. The photo browser and editor always offered a great way to save and organise shots, but Photos now has clever tools that help you to store, edit and share photos unlike ever before.

It starts with advanced artificial intelligence that analyses your library and works out where every shot was taken, who was in the photo and what sort of scene you captured. It uses this information to sort your photos in new ways, and cluster together similar photos in Memories. Photos can have special images ready for you at the click of a button.

New Memories tab

This new tab enables you to see a selection of curated photos that have been gathered for you based on things like location data, the people involved and the images themselves.

Places album

Places makes a welcome return to Photos after being dropped from iPhoto, and it enables you to view all your images on a map. This is great for reminiscing over your trips and holidays.

Intelligent search

Photos now analyses every photo, so you can use intelligent searches to find the image you're looking for. Search 'horses', for example, to find images that Photos thinks contain horses.

People album

Advanced facial recognition now automatically recognises people in every photo and works out which shots contain which people. Find these shots in the People album.

Are these features just for Mac?
No way! All of these features have made their way over to iPhone and iPad with iOS 10, and have extra features you won't even find on the Mac.

Inside your new Messages app

How Messages has livened up the way you communicate

Get drawings
If your friend has an Apple Watch, they can now send you a Digital Touch drawing, and it will appear in the Messages app just like any other short video

Special messages
Friends using an iPhone running iOS 10 can send messages that affect the whole window for more impact – and they will certainly look great on a Mac!

In-line videos
When your friend sends you a link to an amusing video, you can just click the video to watch it within the Messages app, rather than having it open up in Safari

Bigger emoji
If you're sending between one and three emojis to a friend, they can now automatically be sent in a much larger format when you hit send for extra impact

Respond with feeling
You can use the new Tapbacks feature in Messages, which puts one of six icons on a message – such as a thumbs up or a question mark – to make responding faster

Find and discover your favourite songs

Apple Music has been completely redesigned for Mac

While Apple Music was great if you wanted access to hundreds of thousands of songs with a click, the interface in its first iteration could be a little confusing. Now though, Apple has reworked its Apple Music interface to make it easier for you to discover new songs and find your favourites. The revamped For You tab gives you access to new songs and playlists, curated for you by Apple Music's team. You can take a tour through the biggest songs on iTunes in the Browse section, including new releases, exclusives and top charts. Add to this a streamlined MiniPlayer that lets you view lyrics as you listen, and the end result is a much more accessible, user-friendly interface that makes listening to your favourite music so much easier.

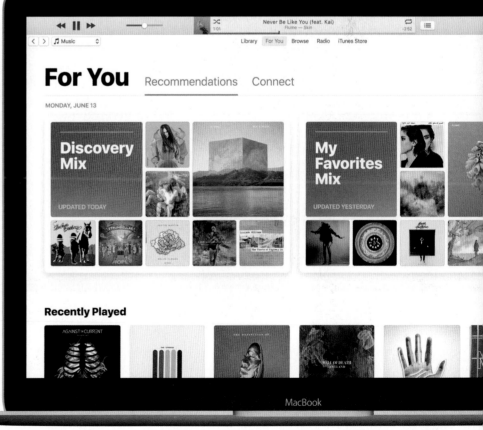

Use your Mac's new Picture-in-Picture mode

Float a video window from Safari or iTunes over your desktop or a full-screen app

Picture-in-Picture came to the iPad in 2015, and proved invaluable. On the Mac it's always been possible, but fiddly to get the same effect. In macOS Sierra though, Apple has made it easier for you to keep watching the big game while you work. The process is really simple too – here's how it works.

Which websites will be available?

It's available for Vimeo, but it's likely that over the next few months many more websites, including YouTube, will add this to their feature set ready for Sierra's public release.

1 Safari or iTunes

You can use Picture-in-Picture mode for videos from iTunes, as well as many videos from Safari. Websites need to use Apple's API for it to work though, so it won't work everywhere right away.

2 Click the button

A new small Picture-in-Picture button appears on the video. Click it and the video will shrink down into the corner of the screen, and an icon will appear where the video was previously playing.

3 Drag and resize

You can resize the video window as you would with any other window, and drag it around the screen. Bear in mind it will snap to the corners, rather than floating freely, however.

Pay for goods with Apple Pay on Safari

Apple Pay is the easiest and safest way to pay for goods

Online shopping has always been preferable on Mac. A bigger screen, mouse-driven experience to access what you want faster – well now it just got a whole lot more swifter and convenient with macOS Sierra thanks to the inclusion of Apple Pay. Whereas previously you had to enter your debit or credit card details to complete your online transactions, with Apple Pay on Mac you can complete your purchases by using Touch ID on your iPhone or by double-clicking the side button on your Apple Watch. As long as the Safari sites you are shopping on support Apple Pay (look for the logo) then you can pay for items without first having to go through the cumbersome process of creating an account for the site and logging in. Amen to that!

Check the receipt
When you click the button, this summary will appear, showing you the things you're buying, the selected delivery address, the shipping method and the price

All in Wallet
Because your payment goes through Apple Pay, you can track all of your spending within the Wallet app on your iPhone to see what you've bought and when

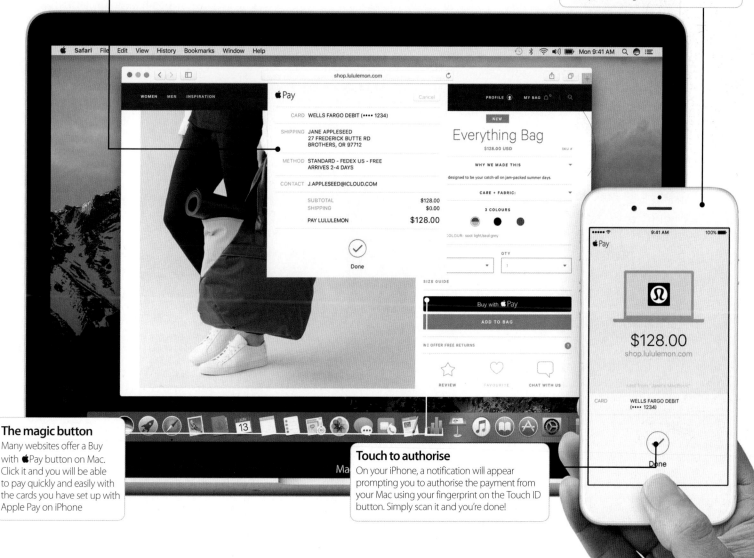

The magic button
Many websites offer a Buy with Pay button on Mac. Click it and you will be able to pay quickly and easily with the cards you have set up with Apple Pay on iPhone

Touch to authorise
On your iPhone, a notification will appear prompting you to authorise the payment from your Mac using your fingerprint on the Touch ID button. Simply scan it and you're done!

Get started

Gain control over your Mac computer with all the essentials of this section

44
Organise your apps

"Your Mac experience can be tailored to your personal preferences"

48
Use the Dashboard

62
Connect to the web

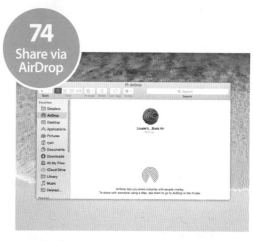

74
Share via AirDrop

Connect to the internet

Gain access to the world wide web by hooking up your Mac to Wi-Fi

To get the most out of your new Mac or MacBook, you will want to connect it to the internet. Luckily, this is a simple process regardless of whether you choose to use either a wired or wireless connection to your router.

If you wish to connect your Mac to the internet with a wired connection, all you need to do is plug one end of an Ethernet cable into your Mac, and the other into your router. If you plan to go wireless, then you don't need any more equipment than your Mac and a wireless-enabled router.

Follow the four simple steps outlined below and you'll soon be able to access a whole host of content: you'll be able to browse the web with Safari, stay in touch with friends and family on Facebook, send emails in the Mail app, download tons of great new apps from the Mac App Store, share videos in iMovie, and much more. A whole world of entertainment awaits you!

OS X Turn Wi-Fi on and start surfing

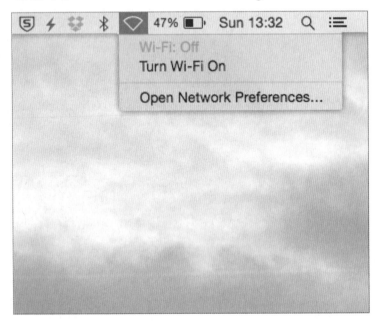

01: Turn it on

Although it should be on by default, your Mac's Wi-Fi may be turned off. If it's off, click on the icon to the left of the time and date in the top bar, then click turn Wi-Fi on.

02: Look for networks

Once you've turned Wi-Fi on, the icon should turn into a greyed-out series of curved lines. Click on it, wait a couple of seconds for a list of available networks to show, then click on your home network.

Network Preferences
How to control your Wi-Fi connection

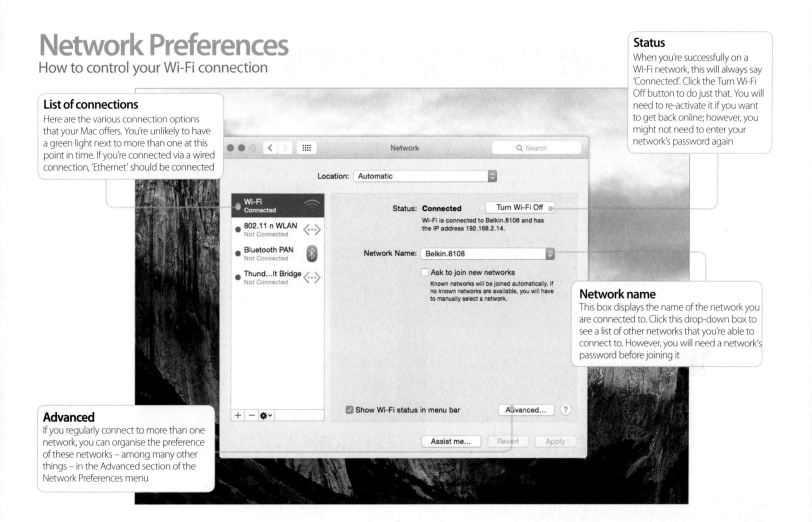

List of connections
Here are the various connection options that your Mac offers. You're unlikely to have a green light next to more than one at this point in time. If you're connected via a wired connection, 'Ethernet' should be connected

Status
When you're successfully on a Wi-Fi network, this will always say 'Connected'. Click the Turn Wi-Fi Off button to do just that. You will need to re-activate it if you want to get back online; however, you might not need to enter your network's password again

Network name
This box displays the name of the network you are connected to. Click this drop-down box to see a list of other networks that you're able to connect to. However, you will need a network's password before joining it

Advanced
If you regularly connect to more than one network, you can organise the preference of these networks – among many other things – in the Advanced section of the Network Preferences menu

03: Connect to your network
For the first time you connect, you'll have to enter your network's passcode, which may be written on the back of your router. Once you've entered it, click 'Join' to connect to the internet.

04: Edit preferences
Now you're connected, the greyed-out curved lines should be black. To edit your connection preferences, click on the icon, then click on 'Open Network Preferences'. You will then be taken to the System Preferences app.

Add a new user account

Share your Mac with the family by creating multiple user accounts

Your brand new Mac is packed with so many great features, both in its software and hardware, that it begs to be used by the whole family. However, you may not want each member changing the computer's settings or having access to your personal files every time they wish to use it. This is where multiple accounts come in.

Not only does having multiple accounts enable you to protect your private data, it also lets you protect children. It's simple to set up an account with Parental Controls, which enable you to limit access to apps and websites, as well as set usage time limits.

There's also a degree of customisation available. Not only can you set your own picture using the iSight camera (so you don't need to settle for stock imagery), you can also set which apps you would like to load as soon as you log in. Multiple user accounts are a great way to keep the whole family safe while still enabling them to enjoy your Mac.

OS X Create and add a new user

01: System Preferences

Click on the System Preferences app (three grey cogs) in the Dock to open it up, and another menu will appear. From this menu, click 'Users & Groups', which is in the fourth category down, 'System'.

02: Add new user

Click the padlock icon to enable changes, and click the + button to add a new user. If setting an account for a child, click the 'New Account' drop-down box and select 'Managed With Parental Controls'.

Parental Controls

Keep a child safe when they're using your Mac

Web tab
The options under this tab enable you to restrict access to certain websites. Apple provides a list of websites that it deems safe, but you are free to create your own custom list of websites

Time Limits tab
This handy tab lets you limit time spent on the Mac. You can set Weekday time limits, Weekend time limits and prevent access to the computer between certain hours on school nights and weekends

Simple Finder
The Simple Finder is a stripped-down version of Apple's desktop environment. There are only three folders on the dock (one for applications, another for documents, and one for sharing), and opening items only takes one click

LOGIN OPTIONS
In the main User & Groups menu, you can change which apps or services open as soon as you log in. To access these options, click the 'Login Items' tab (next to 'Password'). Here, you can click the + symbol to add more apps and services, and untick or tick their checkbox to add them to your login process.

Limit apps
Check this box to limit access to certain apps on your Mac. Tap the arrow next to 'Other Apps' to show a list of all the applications installed on your Mac. Tick the boxes next to the apps that you are happy for your children to use

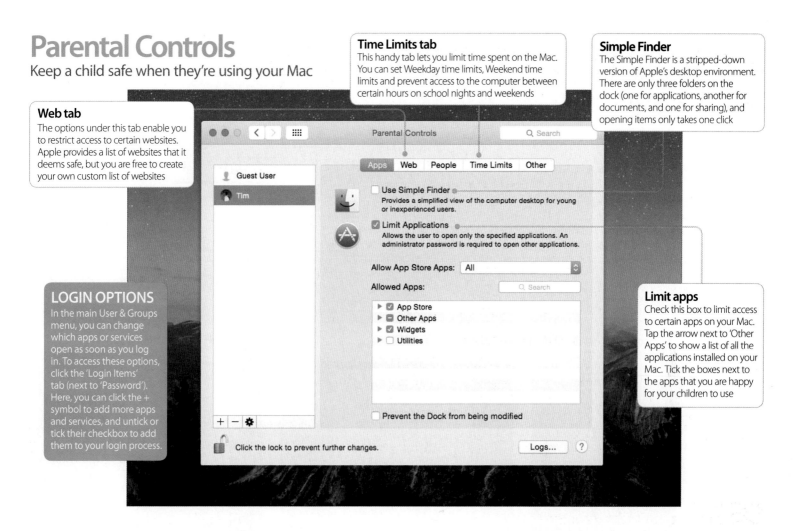

03: Set the picture
After entering a password and clicking 'Create User' you will have a new account on your Mac. To change the account's default picture, click the image next to 'Reset Password…'. To take a picture click the Camera tab, then the camera icon.

04: Parental Controls
After you've set your picture, click 'Open Parental Controls…' to access the parental controls. The tabs across the top grant access to several different ways to limit access to your Mac, including the ability to set time limits on usage.

Get started

Where is everything kept on your Mac?

Put an end to the common problem of keeping track of your files and folders

X It happens to even the most experienced of us – you absent-mindedly put something somewhere and the next thing you know you're searching around wondering where you had it last. It happens to your car keys and it happens to the files and folders on your Mac. Luckily, your Mac makes it easy to

save your stuff in the right place, quickly and often without having to think about it. The key to this is how your Mac handles Home folders, which are a special set of folders that are automatically created for each person that has a user account on your Mac. Know your way around here and you may never get lost on your Mac again.

Find the right folder

Finder sidebar
Every Finder window has shortcuts to the common folders in your Home folder. Click on one to head there.

Head Home
Set new Finder windows to open your Home folder (see steps below) and you'll have common folders to hand.

Keyboard shortcuts
In the Go menu, there are a host of helpful keyboard and menu shortcuts to get you to your favourite folders.

OS X Tweak your Mac to get around quicker

01: A home in every window
To automatically show your Home folder when you open a new Finder window, choose Preferences from the Finder menu.

02: Home sweet home
While in the General tab, choose your personal Home from the 'New Finder windows open' menu to set your preference.

03: Trim Finder sidebars
Click the Sidebar tab and you can choose to turn off any Finder window sidebar shortcuts that you don't think you'll need.

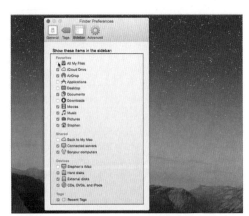

04: Getting ticked off
Just click the checkboxes next to the options to remove them from every sidebar. You can always change your mind later if you wish.

05: Set your own shortcuts
To get your own folder to appear in every Finder sidebar so you can get to it quickly, start by finding the folder on your Mac.

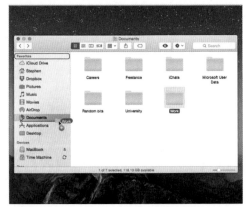

06: Drag it on, drag it off
Click on the folder and drag it into the sidebar and your Mac will pop in a shortcut. To get rid of it, just click on it and drag it back out again.

What's where on your Mac...

Take a moment to snoop around your system and you may quickly become overwhelmed at the array of folders hidden away. Luckily, you only really need to know about just a few of the important ones

Macintosh HD
This is the first folder that contains everything else. It represents the physical storage device inside your Mac, called the Hard Drive.

Applications
Here's where you'll find all of the software that came with your Mac.

Users
This folder contains the Home folders for every person that shares your Mac. This helps to give everyone the ability to have their own settings, music, bookmarks, photos, emails and documents. It doesn't have to all be separate though, and there's a shared folder in here too.

Utilities
This is where you'll find the programs you'll need for making tweaks.

The Library and System folders
With the innards that make your Mac tick exposed inside the Library and System folders, it's best to steer clear of these two!

Your Home folder
This is where you'll find everything that makes your Mac yours – your files, folders, photos, settings and even your desktop. Luckily, it is easy to find, and so this is the starting point for finding or saving your documents. Learn the shortcuts (Cmd+Shift+H) to get here fast.

Shared
Any files stored in here will be accessible to all the users of the Mac – great for sharing documents.

Other people's Home folders
Even if it's your Mac, you won't be able to see what's inside the Home folders of the other users.

Desktop
Anything you dump on your desktop is really kept here inside this folder.
Used by: You, when you want to put a file somewhere quickly.

Documents
This is your general storage area for all your everyday, miscellaneous files and folders.
Used by: Most applications that don't use another folder.

Downloads
When you download a file from the internet and you haven't changed the default folder, it'll be saved to this folder.
Used by: Safari.

Library
The Mac's Library is used to save your preferences, settings and fonts – helping you to personalise your Mac.
Used by: Most applications.

Movies
This is where iMovie will save projects, and so it's where other iLife apps will look for your videos if you want to add them to other projects.
Used by: The iLife apps.

Music
iTunes will create a folder in here for its library, adding any tracks you rip as well as media you buy from the store.
Used by: iTunes.

Pictures
This is the default folder for your pictures, so it is used by iPhoto for its library. Photo Booth also uses it.
Used by: iPhoto and Photo Booth.

Navigate the folders in your Home folder

Your Home folder is your 'safe place' on your Mac – it's where you'll save your files, folders, photos, movies, music and more. Learn your way around it and you'll go a long way toward mastering Mac OS X and your Mac

Public
These last two folders are the only ones that other users can look inside. As the Shared folder does a better job, you'll probably never use them.
Used by: Hardly anyone.

Sites
If you're up for some tricky setting up, you can publish a website from your Mac. Most people won't though.
Used by: Fewer people than the Public folder!

Set up iCloud in OS X

Access your contacts, photos and documents everywhere

When you hear people talking about the cloud, what they mean is using the web to provide various services for computers and internet-connected devices, wherever you may be. iCloud is Apple's online hub for all its devices. Some companies provide general services that anyone can use, but iCloud has been optimised for Apple devices. It is primarily a syncing service, but it also provides an online storage facility for all of your files, apps and music.

The greatest benefit of using iCloud is that it enables email, contacts, calendar appointments, reminders, photos, notes and more to be synced across all your devices, and made available to you no matter where you are or which device you're currently using. You can create a document on your Mac and access it via an iPad, or add a contact on your iPhone and find it instantly appearing on your Mac.

iCloud is very easy to set up, even if you are new to the service. It's one of the first things you will see when you boot up a new Mac or if you log in to a Mac with a new user account. You can even use your iCloud storage like an online folder. Once set up, you can simply drag and drop any file you want into your iCloud Drive on the Mac to upload it, so you can access it anywhere.

iCloud provides 5GB of free online storage and this is more than sufficient for most. Extra space is available for purchase, which is great if you take hundreds of photos or want to store lots of files or music. You can buy 20GB, 200GB, 500GB or even 1TB of space. You can also access all your files even when you're away from your Mac; all you need is a computer with a web browser and you can log in at **www.icloud.com** to access them. Once you've used iCloud with OS X, you may very quickly wonder how you ever lived without it.

> "Once you've used iCloud with OS X, you may very quickly wonder how you ever lived without it"

iCloud Get started with iCloud

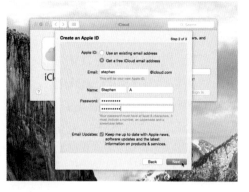

01: Sign in
You can open System Preferences and choose the iCloud section to log in. If you already have an Apple ID, use it here, or click to create a new account.

02: Free email accounts
After entering your birthday, you must add your name and email address. Even if you already have an email account, it's useful to get a free @icloud.com address.

03: Call for security
As part of the sign up process for iCloud, you will be asked to create three security questions. Make these memorable, as they're needed to reset your password.

Get connected to iCloud

Keep everything in sync with your Mac

Space evaders
Keep an eye on this bar at the bottom of the window. It gives you an overall view of the amount of storage space you're currently using – you get 5GB for free

Enable iCloud Drive
Check this box at the top of the list to activate iCloud Drive. This is like an online folder – drag and drop files into it to access them on any device

Manage Family
If several people in your family use iTunes accounts, you can link them all by clicking this button. This way, you can monitor and manage what your kids are buying

Manage your account
This button opens a window that shows which apps are using iCloud and the amount of space they are hogging. Click this if you are running short on storage

CLOUD SPOTTING
Look for the cloud icon in applications; it indicates that some feature or function uses iCloud. For example, if you start TextEdit, you'll see options to create documents on the Mac or in iCloud. Safari has a cloud button too, as do many other apps.

04: Set up iCloud
It couldn't be simpler and the final step is just to tick the iCloud features on for your apps and enable Find My Mac, then OS X will do the rest in seconds.

05: Manage storage
Click System Preferences in the Apple menu and hit the iCloud icon. Click Manage in the bottom right and you can see what accesses iCloud and the space it uses.

06: Update your account
Click Account Details to browse your details. You can change your name and photo, or add a credit card for iTunes, iCloud and other purchases too.

Work with applications

Without applications your Mac would just be a beautiful table decoration. Time to fire up some incredible creative tools…

X It's easy to think of your Mac as a wonderfully creative toolbox, packed to the brim with inspirational tools to finely hone your projects. Those tools are the software saved on your hard drive, the applications. Software, for the most part, is kept in the Applications folder – a shared folder that any user of the Mac can see and open applications from. The beauty of Mac OS X is that each user's version of an application can behave differently and use different files, the same way that each user can have an individual iTunes library. Of course, before you start learning how to use specific applications, it's worth taking a moment to look at how you open, close and switch between them, which is just what we're going to do here.

Five ways you can start an application

You need to open an app before you can start playing with it

01: Launch it from the Dock

Apple places the most used icons in the Dock, where they require a single click to launch. You can add your favourite programs by dragging the app's icon down among the others.

02: In the applications folder

If there's an app you want to launch that's not in the Dock, click Applications in a Finder window sidebar, and scroll through the software list until you find it, then double-click its icon.

03: Double-click a file

Mac OS X is smart enough to launch the right application when you double-click a file that belongs to it. This is often the quickest method if you're working on a specific project.

04: Launch it using Spotlight

Click on the magnifying glass in the top-right corner of the screen, then start typing the name of the app you want to launch. When it appears, and it's highlighted, just hit Return.

05: Plug something in

There are some applications that are smart enough to launch automatically when you need them – iPhoto can launch when you plug in a digital camera, for instance.

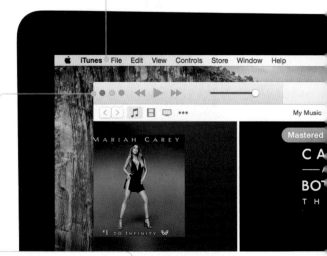

The Application menu
Clicking an application's name in the menu bar gives you a few options for how you see (or don't see) it…
Hide The application's still running, but it will be hidden from view. Click its Dock icon to bring it back.
Hide others Want to focus on just one app? This option clears your screen of all other software.
Show All Brings back all the applications you've hidden.
Quit Closes down the application you're working in, giving you the option to save any unsaved work

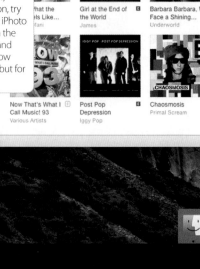

The red button
The great thing about Apple is that there's a wonderful consistency to the products. Once you get used to the way something works you know it's going to work the same way for everything. Except on the very rare occasions it doesn't. For most apps, clicking the red button just closes that window, leaving the application running – go on, try it in iTunes. Now try the same thing in iPhoto and the app automatically quits when the window shuts. Now there is a rhyme and reason for this, and it has to do with how the application works with Windows, but for most people it's just plain confusing!

Five ways you can close an application

Finished playing? Close it down…

01: Application menu
Click on the application's name in the menu bar and choose Quit from the options.

02: Learn the shortcut
Even quicker, press the Cmd key and Q together to gracefully exit the software.

03: Click the Dock icon
Click the Dock icon, keep the mouse button held down, and a menu containing Quit appears.

04: Click the red button
Some apps, like App Store, quit when you close the window by clicking the Red button.

05: Application switcher
Press Cmd+Tab, release Tab, then press it repeatedly to get the app's icon. Then press Q.

Application windows
You can have more than one application open at once and most applications can have more than one window open, which can make for a lot of screen clutter if you're not careful! Luckily you can hide windows, minimise them down to the Dock (click the amber window widget) or use advanced features like Spaces or Exposé to manage your windows

Applications that just won't quit
Sometimes applications run into trouble, and when that happens they'll often just show you a spinning rainbow cursor and refuse to quit. Should that happen to you, just press Cmd+Alt+Esc to bring up the Force Quit window. Click the name of the problem application and then click the Force Quit button to shut it down

Find your way around Mission Control

Delve into the revamped desktop management feature within OS X El Capitan

 With the release of OS X El Capitan, Apple has consciously placed more emphasis on performance over obvious updates. So while revamps to features are not wholesale, this general streamlining does apply to aspects like app workflow.

Mission Control remains central to the way you use your Mac, by providing rapid access to organising apps across a selection of 'spaces' or desktops. The latest iteration of the program makes fairly subtle but useful tweaks, such as placing your app windows together more relatively and giving you the opportunity to arrange them all within a single layer.

The integration with new El Capitan features such as Split View, plus the ability to create new spaces by dragging your apps upwards, all help to maximise the usability experience. Read on for our guide to the best bits of the new and improved Mission Control.

Inside Mission Control

Navigate the core interface elements required for organising your spaces

Spaces thumbnail
Spaces previews help you identify where your apps are. Rollover and click the icons to exit full screen or Split View, or use the 'x' icons to delete and release apps into your current space

The spaces bar
This bar shows tab labels and thumbnails of all the spaces you have created, along with apps in full screen or Split View. You can reorder these by dragging them and navigate between by clicking

Open app windows
Mission Control spreads open apps into a layer, positioned relatively to the original locations. These can then be dragged into the bar and the desired space

ASSIGNING APPS TO CERTAIN SPACES
When launching apps from the Dock, you can assign them specifically to an available space. Click and hold the app icon, choose Options and one of the four choices. All Desktops opens the app in every space; This Desktop uses the current space; Desktop on Display picks a display; while None opens the app in whichever is being used at the time.

Create new spaces
The Add button (+) in the Spaces bar creates a new vacant desktop space, up to a maximum of 16. Alternatively, drag your open app up here to drop it into its own new space

Mission Control Improve your app workflow

01: Ready for launch

Enter Mission Control by either using the third from left Dock icon, Mission Control key (F3), the Ctrl+up shortcut, or swipe up with three or four fingers.

02: Mission control

Open apps are then arranged, with a minimised bar shown across the top to show available 'spaces', including OS X's Dashboard if chosen in Preferences.

03: Give apps spaces

Drag an open app up onto the Spaces bar. This creates a dedicated, full-screen app space for the first app that you can drag a subsequent app into.

04: Split View spaces

Drag a second app into a full-screen space to make it Split View. You can't add any more but may exit Split View by clicking the minimise icon.

05: New desktop spaces

A desktop space can accept multiple apps . You can create these via the Add (+) button on the Spaces bar or dragging apps onto the desktop thumbnail.

06: Navigating spaces

Move between spaces by clicking thumbnails. The Spaces bar places a blue highlight around your current space for keeping track of screen flow.

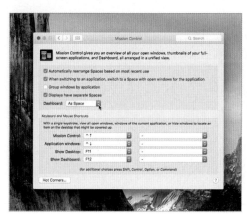

07: Mission Control Preferences

Visit Mission Control in System Preferences. Toggle here to arrange spaces, how they behave, app groups, display and how to show Dashboard.

08: Setting your shortcuts

Mission Control uses shortcuts and gestures by default. You can reassign or add more with the various drop-down menus.

09: Differentiating desktops

If you assign System Preferences to all desktops via the Dock icon, you can change wallpaper within each to make each one more obviously unique.

Organise Launchpad

Make Launchpad work for you with folders and Home screens

Launchpad is another great feature, introduced by Mac OS X Lion, mirroring the functionality of Springboard on iOS. Springboard is the app launcher that you'll find on your iPhone or iPad, which allows you to arrange icons for each of your apps across many Home screens and, if desired, nested into folders.

Every app you install appears automatically on your Home screen, and the same applies for apps installed on your Mac, with each finding its way onto your Launchpad. However, unlike the iPhone,

the Mac App Store isn't the only means of getting apps onto your Mac, so how do you add, remove and control these non-App Store apps?

We've collected together a series of hints and tips to help you get the most out of Launchpad, including taking control of those apps you don't want to appear. We'll also show you how to spice up its appearance with custom icons, organise your apps and navigate around Launchpad quickly. Read on to find out how to tame your OS X Launchpad into submission.

Organise your apps

Control Launchpad to keep things in their rightful place

Gestures
Swipe with two fingers to slide between pages of apps, hold down Opt/Alt to automatically enter the organisation mode (where the apps quiver and allow you to move them around). Do a four-finger reverse pinch to exit Launchpad quickly, or tap Escape on your keyboard

Hide apps
Hide unwanted apps by installing the free System Preferences add-on, which is available from **chaosspace.de/launchpad-control**

Folders
Arrange your apps into folders by clicking and dragging one app onto another. This will create a folder that is automatically named for you. Rename the folder by clicking on its title and typing over the highlighted text

REMOVING NON-APP STORE APPS
One of the limitations of Launchpad is its reluctance to let you remove apps that didn't originate in the Mac App Store. Unless you're brand new to the Mac platform, it's very likely that you've got a reasonable collection of apps that didn't come from here, but when you enter quiver mode, these apps don't have a remove option, so how do you get rid of them? There are a couple of solutions: the easiest is to simply drag all your undesired apps into one folder and hide it on a screen all of its own at the end of the screens. The second is to install the preferences pane found at **http://chaosspace.de/launchpad-control**. This lets you untick apps you don't want to appear, removing the link from Launchpad, but not the app from your computer.

Pages
Each dot represents a different page of apps inside Launchpad. You can navigate between pages by swiping with two fingers, or quickly jump to a page by clicking on the relevant dot to save time

Launchpad Make Launchpad your own

01: Create folders

Drag one app icon onto another. As you release your mouse, the two apps will form a folder, which will be named automatically for you.

02: Move your apps

You can easily re-order your apps within your Launchpad simply by clicking and holding on an app icon and then dragging it into position.

03: Liven it up

Use Emoji icons in your folder names by opening a new TextEdit document, choosing Edit>Emojis & Symbols, and copying then pasting to the Launchpad.

04: Hide unwanted apps

Hide unwanted apps by installing the System Preferences add-on, which is available from **chaosspace.de/launchpad-control**.

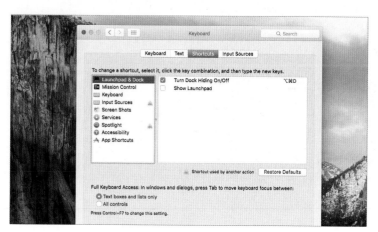

05: Set up a shortcut key

Choose System Preferences>Keyboard, and add a shortcut key into the Keyboard Shortcuts tab.

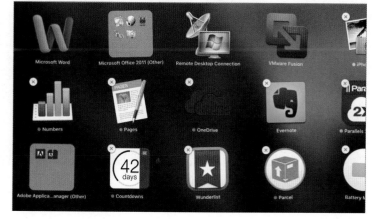

06: Delete apps

To remove apps from your Launchpad, click and hold on an app icon until all the icons quiver. Once they're shaking, click on the 'X' next to an app.

Get started with Dashboard

Learn everything you need to know about how Dashboard can make your life easier

The Dashboard has been present in Mac OS X for several years now, but recently it has seen a lot of changes. At its most basic, the Dashboard is a place in which you can put widgets – which are small, always-on apps that can only be used when in the Dashboard.

Mac OS X has always included some useful widgets that you can use straight out of the box, but independent developers have spent hours creating hundreds more that you can easily install for free from Apple's website.

The Dashboard has recently changed from a screen that overlays your desktop (so that you can see parts of it underneath, but never use it) to a fully separate section to the left of the main Desktop screen. Click on the Dashboard icon in the Dock or use the keyboard shortcut brings it up, and allowing you to play with widgets to your heart's content.

You can change your widget settings by clicking the 'i' that appears whenever you hover over them.

> "At its most basic, the Dashboard is a place in which you can put widgets"

Discover Dashboard
Find out what each standard widget is for

World Clock
Displaying the time from anywhere in the world, adding a few of these lets you keep track of as many time zones as you want to

Safari Webclip
You can add a snapshot of your favourite blog or video by opening the page in the Safari browser and choosing 'Open' in Dashboard

Weather
This weather widget will tell you what it's like anywhere in the world. If you click it once, you can get a weekly forecast of your choice

Calendar
The calendar widget features three columns – today's date, a month view, and a column that displays your Calendar events for today

Translator
The translator widget lets you choose from a wide range of languages, translating text quickly and easily

Stickies
If you're always forgetting things, use Stickies to keep notes. Fonts and colours are changeable, making sure your notes will stand out

Unit Converter
Whatever you need to convert, the Unit Converter widget will do it for you in a pinch. Weight, time, pressure and energy are just a few of the many options for this powerful and useful widget

Tile Game
A simple game widget, the Tile Game is just the tip of the iceberg when it comes to widget-based games. Check out the Apple website to find more

Address Book
This widget allows you to quickly search your computer's contacts to find the person you need, without the need to open the Address Book app

Ski Report
If you're off on holiday to the mountains, and want to check the latest times in your area, you can type a resort name in here and view the conditions of the snow

Dictionary
The Dictionary widget allows you to search for any word quickly, getting you a definition or synonym quickly

ESPN
If you're an American Sports junkie, the ESPN widget is made for you. Get news and scores for hockey, football, baseball and more

Calculator
Small, neat, and much quicker than Lion's app. Typing numbers and symbols is supported to increase productivity

Flight Tracker
Choose an airline, departure city and arrival city to view the status of flights. Incredibly useful if you travel with your Mac

Movies
If you live in the US, you can quickly check the latest times in your area, as well as buy tickets once you know what you want to see

Stocks
If you're financially minded and like to keep an eye on stocks, this will help do just that. Input your companies and away you go

Key features
Starting the Dashboard

Two ways to access Dashboard

Lion made it even easier to access your Dashboard. Since that version of OS X was released, Dashboard has become a space to the left of your main desktop that is there whenever you need it. Getting there is easy. You can swipe your fingers quickly to the right on your Trackpad or Magic Mouse and watch the Dashboard slide onto your screen. Alternatively, open Mission Control and click on the Dashboard thumbnail.

Adding new widgets

While there are only four widgets on the screen when you first open the Dashboard, there are a lot more available. Click on the '+' symbol in the bottom left corner of the screen and a screen will appear showing all of the available widgets. To add one, click on it and it will appear on your Dashboard and you can click and hold and drag it into position. See the opposite page to find out what each widget can do.

Arrange your widgets

When you first see your Dashboard, there should be four widgets in the middle of the screen; the Weather, World Clock, Calculator and Calendar. They certainly aren't stuck in those positions; if you want to move them around, you can click and drag them to a different area of the Dashboard. Unlike normal windows, there isn't a bar you have to click to move each widget – clicking and dragging from anywhere will work.

Manage your widgets

If you wish to remove widgets then the process is just as simple. Click on the '-' symbol and a 'X' will appear in the corner of every widget – click this to delete it. Once done, click on '-' again to return to normal. To download new widgets that aren't currently on your Mac, click the '+' symbol followed by the 'More Widgets' button at the bottom of the window, and choose from the hundreds of free choices on the Apple website.

Get to know Notification Centre

An invaluable central place to view all your important alerts, updates and more on your Mac

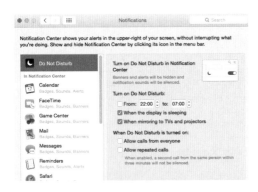

The Notification Centre is a central focus for change on your Mac, recording new happenings and occurrences. It's a place where you can find information regarding updates for your apps and you can also see information on new mail that has arrived. Reminders are another area that the Notification Centre handles, as well as information from the likes of FaceTime, Game Center, Calendar, plus messages from other third-party apps. The Notification Centre can be configured by yourself, however, so it's not set in stone. You can tell the Mac just how you want to see your alerts, in what style and format and for how long you want these alerts to remain on the screen. This focuses on the visual end of the Centre, but you can also include sounds in that suite of features too. Let's take a closer look at this useful facility.

Explore the interface

Manage your alerts and updates

Notification Centre
This main window is placed on the right of the screen and is normally hidden from view but can be triggered to open, revealing your alerts, updates and news

Timing
Next to each alert you will see a relative time/date to inform you when the alert arrived. On the desktop the notice badge alerts provide an alternative method of bringing change to your attention

DO NOT DISTURB
If you are busy or need to concentrate, then regular messages and alerts will not help. Swipe the Do Not Disturb switch to On, at the top of the Notification Centre, to remove them all. Also, every time you get a notification an interactive bubble appears at the top-right-hand side of your screen. You can automatically reply to any message you get by hovering over the bubble and then pressing the Reply button.

Header
Each app provides a heading and icon, then the alerts, news or updates underneath. If you want to remove the information for that app, click the X next to the header

Notification Centre Master the Notification Centre in OS X

01: Open Notification Centre

To open the Notification Centre, click on System Preferences. On the first line, at the far right, is the Notification Centre icon, so click it to open.

02: Choose an app

Pick which app you want to modify by looking in the left panel. Scroll the available list until you find your desired app and then click it.

03: Choose style

You can choose from one of three possible styles: None; Banner (appears for a short time); and Alerts (stays until you remove them).

04: Show in Centre

If you click on the Show in Notification Centre option box then the alerts will always appear in the Notification Center on the right side of the screen.

05: Recent items

Next to Show in Notification Centre, click to see 1, 5, 10 or 20 Recent Items. This denotes how many older alerts will be retained in the Notification Centre.

06: Badge icons

Click on the Badge app icon to enable alerts and/or updates to show badges on the icon of the app in the Dock. The red icon has a white alert number.

07: Play sound

Tick the Play Sound for Notifications box to ask the Mac to play its alert sound when you receive an alert, update or news item.

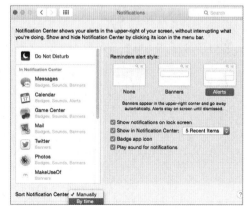

08: Sort notifications

Clicking Sort Notification Centre will produce a pop-up menu with two options presented to sort Notification Centre manually or by time.

09: Order apps

If you aren't happy with the order of the apps offered in the Notification Centre then you can click and drag an app to rearrange their order.

Set up widgets in Notification Centre

Extend Notification Centre's functionality by using time-saving widgets that'll enhance your lifestyle

Notification Centre was introduced to Macs back in Mountain Lion and for the past couple of years has served as an at-a-glance method of viewing everything that's going on in your world. It gives you direct access to all your social interactions and business appointments. One major change in OS X Yosemite 10.10 was the introduction of the Today view, which – just like in iOS – gives you a run-down of your day's events from Calendar entries, Reminders, weather forecast and so on. Your entire day is laid out for you.

What's even better is that you can add widgets to your Today view by hitting Edit, for a fully customisable and personal Notification Centre. There are widgets to suit any interest or need, so you can modify the Notification Centre to your personal preferences. Essentially, Notification Centre's usefulness has been improved exponentially. We're going to guide you through setting up and using third-party widgets to Notification Centre, giving any new OS X user a time-saving method of checking vital information in no time at all.

Notification Centre widgets

Up close with your pimped out Notification Centre

In-depth info
Most widgets are expandable and provide even more information with just a couple of clicks – just like the Weather widget shown here. Time to wrap up warm

Notifications
Don't forget the traditional Notifications tab, which lists all of your various unseen notifications and enables you to respond straight from Notification Centre

Do Not Disturb
Taking your Mac into an important meeting? Sleeping with it under the pillow? Just activate Do Not Disturb, set a time period for silence and tweak the settings as you wish

App Store
The ultimate place for an essential list of compatible apps can be found via this App Store shortcut in Edit mode under the Today view

THE END FOR DASHBOARD?
When widgets for Notification Centre were announced at WWDC, everyone shared the same thought: this is the end for Dashboard, Apple's home of the simple widget. Well, it still exists but its days are surely numbered. Using a widget in Notification Centre makes a lot of sense, is quick and easy, and is supported by a thriving community of third-party developers.

Notification Centre Customise the Today view

01: Basic setup
Access Notification Centre through a three-lines icon in the top-right corner of your menu bar. Your basic Today view is very useful but limited.

02: Mac App Store
A host of great apps already support the widget feature and there's a list on the Mac App Store's Featured page. Take a look and get downloading!

03: Edit tab
The Edit button at the bottom of the Today view powers up Notification Centre. Click it and you're presented with a new row of compatible widgets.

04: Click the plus
To add a widget click on the green plus sign next to its name. Click Done in the bottom-right and the widget is instantly added to your Today view.

05: Use a widget
Most widgets require a bit of personalising. The World Clock, for example. Hit the 'i' button and add a face by typing in a place and hit Done.

06: Add social accounts
Other widgets require you to add account details, like the Social widgets. Click Add Account and follow the steps to get your account running.

07: Time saver
Now you won't need the app or a browser. Send a Facebook update or tweet a post with all the usual additions, right from Notification Centre.

08: Reorder
Notification Centre lets you reorder the widgets on your Today view. Click and drag to reorder and banish widgets by hitting the red minus icon.

09: System Preferences
Edit mode leads you to System Preferences via the cog in the bottom-right. Customise how you receive notifications from your widgets here.

Get started with Siri on Mac

Siri is as useful on a Mac as it is on an iPhone

 Siri has almost taken on a status similar to Hoover and iPhone in its ability to be recognised by name even if another service is used. It is capable, fast and for many iPhone and iPad users has slowly crept into their daily workflows to the point that using a mobile device just wouldn't feel the same without it. The really good news is that Siri works in almost the same way on a Mac thanks to macOS Sierra, and it even comes with some extra functionality to boot. The wide-ranging nature of the implementation is impressive and so is the set-up process, which is almost non-existent, so it shouldn't take you long to start enjoying Siri on your Mac, just as you do on your iPhone today.

"Siri works in almost the same way on a Mac thanks to macOS Sierra"

Do almost anything with Siri

The personal assistant now lives on your Mac

Siri settings
There are some settings for you to play around with to help you change the style of the voice and to set up Siri keyboard shortcuts. There is nothing unnecessary included in the settings screen.

Siri hasn't aged
The main Siri interface looks very similar to what you will be used to on your iPhone or iPad. It offers visual and audible feedback to help you understand the results instantly.

Manage apps
Some Siri questions will open an associated app to give you the answer you need in greater detail. For example, asking for a route will immediately open the macOS Maps app.

CHANGE SYSTEM SETTINGS
Siri on a Mac is extremely flexible and has the ability to directly interact with the hardware itself. For example, you can say "Turn Bluetooth off" and it will be done immediately with a small panel appearing. This lets you turn it back on if needed and means that most of the hard-to-find settings are now easily accessible.

Pin the answers
You can click the '+' icon in a Siri answer to pin it to the notifications panel. This lets you get the info you need and then refer to it when the time is right.

Use Siri on your Mac Learn how to make life easier with Siri

01: Enable Siri

Enter Mission Control by either using the third from left Dock icon, Mission Control key (F3), the Ctrl+up shortcut, or swipe up with three or four fingers.

02: Set it up

Open apps are then arranged, with a minimised bar shown across the top to show available 'spaces', including OS X's Dashboard if chosen in Preferences.

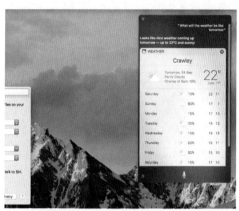

03: Ask a question

Drag an open app up onto the Spaces bar. This creates a dedicated, full-screen app space for the first app that you can drag a subsequent app into.

04: Save the answer

Drag a second app into a full-screen space to make it Split View. You can't add any more but may exit Split View by clicking the minimise icon.

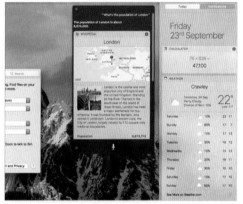

05: Access more detail

A desktop space can accept multiple apps . You can create these via the Add (+) button on the Spaces bar or dragging apps onto the desktop thumbnail.

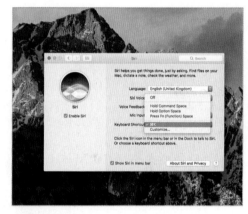

06: Set keyboard shortcut

Move between spaces by clicking thumbnails. The Spaces bar places a blue highlight around your current space for keeping track of screen flow.

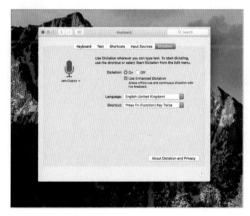

07: Use dictation

Visit Mission Control in System Preferences. Toggle here to arrange spaces, how they behave, app groups, display and how to show Dashboard.

08: Say Hey

Mission Control uses shortcuts and gestures by default. You can reassign or add more with the various drop-down menus.

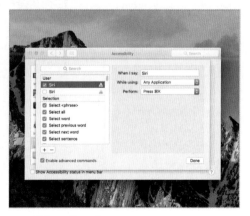

09: The final setup

If you assign System Preferences to all desktops via the Dock icon, you can change wallpaper within each to make each one more obviously unique.

Take advantage of Spotlight

Learn all about Spotlight's new features and advanced search capabilities

When you need to find an app, document or other file, Spotlight has long been the go-to tool for Mac users. An updated version of this essential feature is in OS X El Capitan, boasting some great new aspects and even better searches than before.

For example, Spotlight can be resized and moved around the screen almost like any other regular window, which prevents it from getting in the way of other apps on the screen and shows more search results. The range of Spotlight's searches is wider than before and it can find even more content on the web than ever.

There is no need to fire up Safari when performing a web search, when you can hit Cmd+Space and enter a Spotlight search (which will now search the web as well as your computer). It also has a better understanding of search queries, too, and can find items related to a phrase written as you would speak it naturally.

Intelligent Spotlight searches

Get much more from Spotlight searches

Top Hits
The Top Hit is Spotlight's best guess and it is indeed the Harry Potter book in this case. The result is an email and the icons next to each result indicate the type of item

Jump to here
Search results are organised into sections to make them easier to navigate. Jump from one section to another section by holding down Command and pressing the up and down arrow keys

Related information
This really highlights Spotlight's ability to find not only direct results like the top hit, but related information. It obviously looked up the author and displayed another book from her, which is clever

Resize and move
The window can be moved by dragging the top bar and the top and bottom can be clicked and dragged up or down to make the window bigger or smaller. The width is fixed, though

CONFIGURE SPOTLIGHT
The results that Spotlight shows can be configured by going to System Preferences and clicking Spotlight. Tick the items that you want to see results for and clear the ticks against anything that you don't want to see. Ticking everything might show too much, so use the list to filter the search results to show important ones.

Spotlight Get to know Spotlight

01: Search with Spotlight

Click the Spotlight icon on the menu bar and enter what want to find on the Mac or the web, such as The Martian. There are books, movies and more.

02: Move Spotlight

Clicking the music link opens the iTunes Store. Open Spotlight and click and drag the window to any place on the screen like a regular app window.

03: Search for videos

Add 'video' to the end of the search term and it changes everything. Now the results include links to movies on the web. In this case, the YouTube trailer.

04: Get the weather

Search for 'weather' and the forecast for your local area displays. You can just as easily see weather forecasts for any where. Just add the location.

05: Expand the window

Sometimes there is too much information to fit in the Spotlight results window. It's easy to resize it. Click and drag the top and bottom edges.

06: Get sports info

Spotlight can now show sports information such as upcoming fixtures and match results. Just type the name of a football team or match to see the results.

07: Spotlight contacts

Spotlight can be accessed from within the Contacts app. Open Contacts and select a person in the list. Go to the Edit menu and select Spotlight: 'name'.

08: Intelligent searches

A degree of artificial intelligence has been built into Spotlight and it can understand more than you might expect. For example, search for 'emails from name'.

09: Use dates

Dates can also be used in searches. Suppose you want to see the photos you took in January. Just type 'photos from January' in Spotlight.

Inside System Preferences: Personal

Learn how to tune and tinker with the inner workings of your Mac by following this simple, four-part guide to System Preferences. First up: the Personal settings…

 Many Mac users are happy to leave their Mac set up the same way it was the day they opened the box. That's fair enough – after all, why fix what isn't broken? However, if you're prepared to take a few minutes to delve into the wealth of settings at your fingertips, you may just find a few that could change the way you work, make your Mac a safer place or just spruce the ol' gal up a little. In the first of a four-part guide, we're going to take you, icon by icon, through the top row of the System Preferences window: the Personal settings…

Security

Energy Saver

By setting your Mac to require a password when waking it from sleep or screen saver, your Mac will automatically lock while you're away. You can also set it to only respond to a certain remote control.

FileVault

By using FileVault, you can automatically encrypt every file on your Mac – great for security-conscious laptop users worried about losing their computer, and the sensitive data it contains.

Firewall

It's no myth that Macs are safer on the internet than Windows-based computers, but if you'd rather be safe than sorry you can turn on the Firewall to monitor and block potentially dangerous connections from the net.

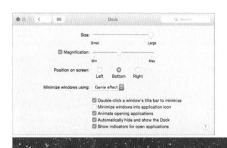

Dock

With these settings, you can easily control how the Dock (the bar of icons along the bottom of your screen) looks and behaves.

Desktop & Screen Saver

Desktop

Set the background picture on your desktop to one of the Apple-supplied images, one of your own photos from iPhoto or one you've downloaded from the internet.

Screen Saver

Set an animation that automatically starts when your Mac hasn't been used for a while. Choose from one of Apple's, or automatically create a slideshow from your iPhoto albums.

Mission Control

General

Sometimes you can't find the window you need among the many you have open. Mission Control provides a handy overview of all your open windows and applications all arranged in a unified view. You can tailor the views and shortcuts here.

Hot Corners

Accessible from the Mission Control pane is the 'Hot Corners' settings. You can move your cursor into a corner of your screen to trigger certain actions, such as screensavers and sleep mode. You can determine what corner performs which action here.

Scroll bar controls

With a scrolling mouse, you may never have used the scroll bars on the edge of every window, but there may still be settings here that you'll find extremely useful – such as the Jumping options

Text smoothing options

Without smoothing the words on your screen can appear harsh and jagged, but you might find text too fuzzy to read comfortably at smaller sizes. You can fine-tune the effect here

Search System Preferences

If you know there's an option you'd like to change but can't remember where it is, try entering its name into this search box to see matching icons dynamically highlighted

General

In this pane, you'll find the settings that affect how your windows and menus appear. You have the choice between the usual Blue theme, with shiny blue controls and red, amber and green window widgets, or – if you find all the colour distracting – you can switch to the Graphite theme where all the controls are grey instead.

Language & Region

General

For most users, this will come preset, but you can quickly change the language of menus and controls in the left-hand pane of this screen.

Advanced

Dates, prices or times not displaying the way that you would like? You can change how your Mac automatically formats numbers by clicking Advanced on the Language & Regions page. Presets for most regional variations are here.

Text

Click Keyboard Preferences from the Language & Region panel to find the Text options. You can set your Spell Check options here, and also set your Mac to replace certain typed shortcuts with special symbols, like (c) for ©. This only works in supported applications.

Keyboard

While you're here, click the Keyboard tab. The thing most users will find useful in this section of System Preferences is turning on the Keyboard and Character Viewer, which gives you a map of those hard-to-find symbols on your keyboard, like é, ü or °.

Notifications

In Notification Centre

In this panel, you will be able to determine what apps alert you in your Notification Centre and change the order by dragging the apps around.

Alert style

Click on a listed app and then you will be able to determine how the alerts appear on screen, such as banners and alerts that pop-up on screen.

Inside System Preferences: Hardware

Get to grips with the technology inside your Mac by following this simple four-part guide to the System Preferences. Part two: get your hands dirty with the Hardware settings…

 The simplicity of Mac OS X means that you don't have to become an expert on computer hardware to enjoy using your Mac. For most peripherals, you can just plug in and play; at the worst, you may have to install the occasional driver. However, with the improvements made in recent version of Mac OS X, even these installations are becoming fewer and farther between. This ease of use doesn't mean there aren't any settings to fiddle with, though – System Preferences has a whole row of icons dedicated to fine-tuning the hardware settings of your Mac, and a few well-chosen tweaks could vastly improve the way you work.

Displays

Make sure you're using the optimum viewing settings to get the most from your monitor

Display

Everything seem a little small on screen? The higher up the list you set the resolution, the more pixels and screen space you'll have, but everything looks a little smaller as a result.

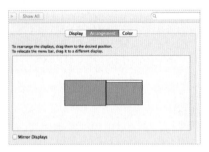

Arrangement

If you're sporting more than one monitor for your Mac, this panel lets you tell your computer how they are positioned and which one you want the Menu bar to appear on.

Colour

Ensure you're seeing the correct colours by either selecting the correct Display profile or, even better, by clicking the Calibrate button to create a bespoke setting.

Schedule

Want your Mac to be on when you wake up or get home from work? Use the Energy Saver schedule to set when your Mac turns on, turns off, goes to sleep or wakes up

CDs & DVDs

It sounds a simple thing, but it makes a great deal of sense to set up how you'd like your Mac to behave when you slide a disc into the drive. Want blank CDs to appear on the desktop? Just set the blank CD action to 'Open Finder'. Don't want the DVD player to open when you pop in a movie disc? Just choose 'Ignore' from the video DVD menu, or set it to open in Front Row if that's how you prefer to watch your films.

Energy Saver

Possibly the most useful of this row of preferences, the Energy Saver settings do much more than cut down your electricity bill. The Computer Sleep slider sets how long you'd like your Mac to stay on when you're not using it, while a second slider lets you set the same for just the Display.

Keyboard

Keyboard

Considering how much of the time you spend sitting in front of your Mac, you also spend time tapping away at your keyboard, so it's good to make sure you've got it set up perfectly. If you're a slow typist then increasing the 'Delay Until Repeat' setting is an especially good idea if you often find yourself typing repeating letters.

Keyboard Shortcuts

Mac OS X comes crammed with many keyboard shortcuts that can speed up how you work, saving your hand a trip to the mouse or Trackpad. Not only can you discover what they all are from this pane, you can also tweak and change them to better suit your fingertips – a great way to personalise your Mac for the way you work.

Printers & Scanners

With every new version of Mac OS X, Apple has significantly improved the printer installation experience. So much so that many users will never need to visit the Print & Scan preference pane – simply plug in your printer and most times it will just work. That said, it's still useful to set your default paper size or check the amount of ink in your printer by clicking the Options & Supplies button.

"If you're the arty type and use a graphics tablet, you might want to have a play with the handwriting recognition built into Mac OS X"

Sound
Sound Effects

Your Mac makes a number of small noises to give you feedback on certain events. Choose which ones you'd like to hear, and how loud you'd like them to be.

Output

On most Macs there are a number of ways to pipe the audio out – through headphones, the built-in speakers or through a digital optical cable, for example. You can choose which one to use from this pane.

Input

The audio input options are less useful to most users, until you decide to try Skype, record a movie voice-over or experiment with GarageBand. Choosing the right input device will depend on the equipment you use, but it is vital for a great result.

Ink

If you're the arty type and use a graphics tablet, then you might want to have a play with the handwriting recognition that's built into Mac OS X. Ink allows you to enter text using your pen and tablet instead of the keyboard, and it can be great for taking notes. You can also set up gestures to control your Mac with the pen.

Mouse & Trackpad

The pane that you see here will depend on whether you use a laptop with a Trackpad, a Magic Mouse, Mighty Mouse or a third-party mouse. As with the keyboard settings, considering how much time you spend controlling a cursor, it's important to get these settings perfect – especially the tracking and double-click speeds.

Learn your gestures
As multi-touch devices, like the Magic Mouse or the Trackpad on your laptop, improve the way you get around your Mac, you'll find yourself faced with more and more gestures and actions. You can customise them so the different buttons suit you

Inside System Preferences: Internet & Wireless

Get to grips with the technology inside your Mac by following this simple, four-part guide to the System Preferences. Part three: networking and syncing

 There's one aspect that sets the computers of today far apart from those we were using just ten years ago: networks. Back in 2000, the internet was only just starting to become commonplace, and if you did have it then you probably only had it on one computer in the house (which wasn't really a problem, as most houses only had one computer). Now, with the advent of easy Wi-Fi and cheaper computers (plus iPods and iPhones), many houses have a handful of connected devices sharing the airwaves and, with a little setup, sharing their connections, files and data too. The Internet & Wireless row of icons in System Preferences is all about your Networks – local and worldwide – how you interact with them and how you choose to share across them, be it sharing your files, screen, printer or even disc drive.

Network

For most users, this should hopefully be one of those 'set it and forget it' preference panes, if you ever need to set it at all. With most modern networks, you should find your Mac just connects and configures itself. Bliss.

Bluetooth

Check out the status of the Bluetooth peripherals you have connected to your Mac. To add a new Bluetooth device, like a mouse, keyboard or phone, click the '+' button.

"You should find your Mac just connects and configures itself"

Sharing
DVD or CD Sharing

Share your DVD drive with a Mac that either has a broken drive or doesn't have one at all, like the MacBook Air or the Mac mini server.

Screen Sharing
Allow another computer (or iPhone) on your network to see your screen, and even control your Mac remotely.

File Sharing
Make files in certain folders available to other computers on your network. You can control who sees what.

Printer Sharing
With the tick of a box, you can share any printer connected to your Mac with any other local computer.

Scanner Sharing
With Mac OS X Yosemite, this feature has now been incorporated into the Printer sharing settings.

Internet Sharing
Share your internet connection with another computer by ticking the box and selecting the correct ports.

Remote Login
For those users happy typing commands into Terminal, this setting allows remote login to the Mac.

iCloud
Account Details

Sign in with your iCloud details to be able to sync details, files, music and movies across all of your devices.

Sync

Syncing across iCloud allows multiple Macs and iPhones, even those in different locations, to share the same bookmarks, address books, calendars and more.

Manage

The iCloud is your virtual hard drive on the internet. You can use it to store photos, movies and files. This preference pane lets you check your space – you are provided with 5GB as standard but can purchase more if you need it.

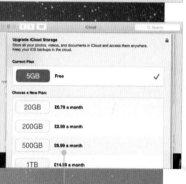

View Account

You can use this option to check that your existing account details are correct or edit them to reflect any changes in your address or credit card information. You can also upgrade your iCloud account with more storage.

Remote Management

A step-up from Screen Sharing, Remote Management allows system-level control of your Mac from afar.

Remote Apple Events

For the real power users, Remote Apple Events allows your Mac to be automated by other computers.

Purchase more space

Your iCloud account comes with 5GB of free space as standard, but if you come to realise that you require more, then click on 'Manage Account' and then click 'Change' next to the Storage option and purchase anything up to 50GB in storage space

Stay safe

You don't want to let just anyone send your files over Bluetooth, especially if you use a laptop in crowded areas like airports. To be safe, tick both 'Require pairing' boxes and leave the 'When' options as 'Ask What to Do'

Bluetooth Sharing

Share photos, ringtones and more with a mobile phone using Bluetooth Sharing to create a short range network to pass files across.

Get started

Inside System Preferences: System

Get to grips with the technology inside your Mac by following this final part of our guide to System Preferences. In this section, delve into the final row – the System settings

The System settings, like the Network settings above them, get deep down and dirty into the depths of OS X. Many of the changes affect all users of the Mac, and it's here where you'll discover the tools you need to control which users can do what. It's also where you'll find Accessibility, the first place you should go if you have physical difficulties that make it hard for you to enjoy using your Mac.

Date & Time

Always be sure that your Mac's clock is bang on time by setting it to automatically stay synchronised with Apple's time servers over the internet.

Time Zone

Let your Mac know where you are in the world by clicking the map near where you are, then choosing the closest city to you from the pop-up menu at the bottom of the screen.

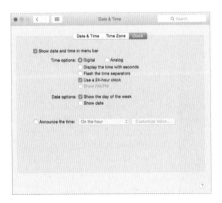

Clock

Set how your Menu bar displays the date and time. If Menu bar space is at a premium then you can choose to see a tiny analogue clock, or even get rid of it completely and have your Mac announce the time on the hour, every hour.

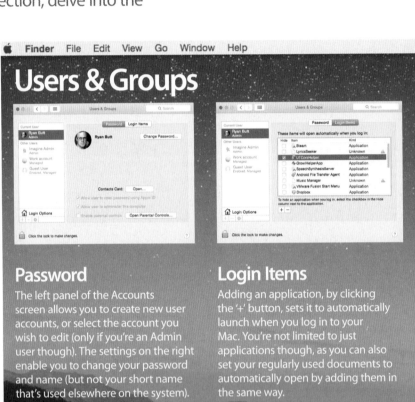

Users & Groups

Password

The left panel of the Accounts screen allows you to create new user accounts, or select the account you wish to edit (only if you're an Admin user though). The settings on the right enable you to change your password and name (but not your short name that's used elsewhere on the system).

Login Items

Adding an application, by clicking the '+' button, sets it to automatically launch when you log in to your Mac. You're not limited to just applications though, as you can also set your regularly used documents to automatically open by adding them in the same way.

Dictation & Speech

Dictation

Wherever you can type text on your Mac, you can now speak it instead. By activating this feature and using your Mac's built-in microphone, you can dictate to your machine and then the recording will be digitally sent to Apple and converted into text. Read more about it in the pane itself.

Text to speech

Not only can you talk to your Mac, it can talk straight back at you. Text to Speech can give you valuable audio feedback when your Mac requires your attention, speaking alert boxes and more. You can also choose your Mac's voice from a wide range of styles and speeds.

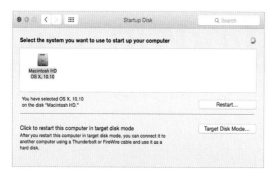

Startup Disk

For power users with different versions of Mac OS X installed across multiple hard drives, this pane enables you to pick the drive you'd like to start from.

Time Machine

Mac OS X comes with what is arguably the best 'set it and forget it' backup utility: Time Machine. Turn it on, select a disk and then rest assured that your data is safe.

"You can choose how often you would like it to check for updates or run a manual check yourself"

Software Update

Software Update runs automatically to ensure your Mac is always running the most up-to-date version of any Apple software you have installed, including OS X, iPhoto, iMovie, Pages and more. It lives inside the App Store app, but you can access Software Update via the App Store tab in System Preferences.

Accessibility

This pane houses all of the options to make the Mac much easier to use if you are visually impaired, hard of hearing or find it difficult to hold down multiple keys simultaneously. Here, you will find options relating to the display, keyboard, mouse and more, to tailor your Mac to your needs.

Tweak your trackpad settings in System Preferences

Learn how to change the settings in System Preferences to master multi-touch gestures

 If multi-touch gestures, introduced with Snow Leopard, are the cornerstone of the OS X experience, then the trackpad can certainly be seen as the bricks and mortar that holds it all together. Without the built-in multi-touch trackpad on the MacBook Pro or MacBook Air, or the amazing wireless Magic Trackpad, OS X and its myriad new features wouldn't run half as smoothly.

The trackpad settings pane in System Preferences helps to make that experience even better by allowing you to decide which gestures perform what action, as well as playing you a handy video of exactly how to perform them. It means you can make the trackpad work exactly how you want it to and tailor it to your needs. In this tutorial, we'll show you how to get the best out of this little-known feature in order to make the most of your OS X experience. It's an easy process that will soon have you finding your way around your Mac with smooth moves that suit you.

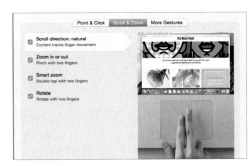

Using the preferences

Make the trackpad settings suit your needs with this window

Tabs
Different trackpad settings are grouped under three different tabs – this makes finding exactly what you want to adjust a lot easier and quicker. It also helps to de-clutter what can often be confusing preference panes

Making settings simple
Recent versions of OS X have improved the UI of its trackpad settings by spacing out different settings and making it clear which ones relate to which gesture with the use of highlights, arrows and videos

MASTERING GESTURES
In order to get the most out of OS X, it's a good idea to get used to the gestures that will save you time. For example, pinching with your thumb and three fingers with a claw-like movement will bring up Launchpad, while pushing three fingers upwards will bring up Mission Control. Both gestures allow you to speed up things like organising your desktop and launching apps.

Tracking problems?
If your Magic Trackpad is slow or unresponsive, your first port of call should be the tracking speed slider in the trackpad settings. If that doesn't make any difference, try replacing the batteries in your trackpad and reconnecting

Video previews
Even if you don't want to change any of your trackpad settings, the video previews in System Preferences can really help you master some of the more tricky multi-touch gestures. They're time-savers and worth learning

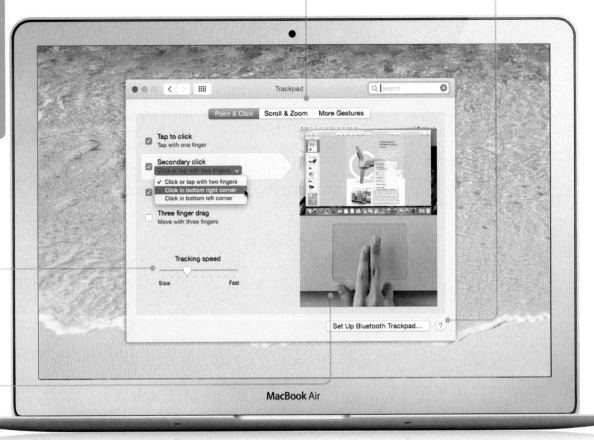

System Preferences Tweak your trackpad settings

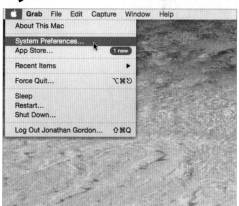

01: System Preferences

Click on the Apple logo in the menu bar, then click on System Preferences. Here you'll find all the settings for your Mac.

02: Find the icon

Click on the Trackpad icon in System Preferences – this is known as a preferences pane. When you install apps, they'll create preference panes here.

03: Check them

Trackpad settings are displayed as checkboxes; check or uncheck them to activate or deactivate the settings. A video description is included to help you.

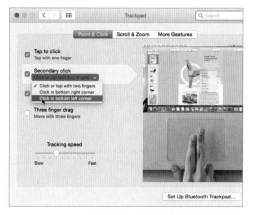

04: Change the gesture

Under some settings, you can change the gesture that controls them. Click on the drop-down menu and choose the gesture that best suits you.

05: Hover and preview

A short video animation is displayed to help you understand how to perform different gestures. Simply hover over the gesture's name to preview.

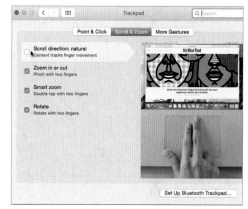

06: Different directions

Uncheck 'Scroll direction: natural' to revert two-finger scrolling to pre-Lion behaviour. Since then, content follows your finger movement.

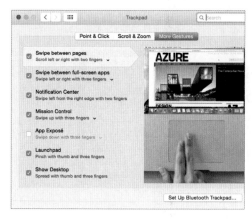

07: More Gestures

Under the More Gestures tab you'll find some of the more complex gestures. Make use of the videos to master these new features.

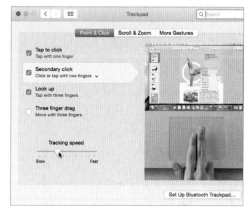

08: Tracking Speed

Drag the Tracking Speed slider to adjust the sensitivity to your finger movement. The faster on the slider, the more responsive it will be.

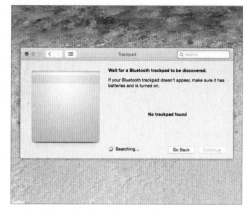

09: Magic Trackpads

If you own a Magic Trackpad, set it up by clicking 'Set Up Bluetooth Trackpad' in the bottom corner of the Trackpad settings window.

Set up and use Split View

Learn how to place two full-screen apps side-by-side with
OS X's new multitasking feature

 One of the many new features in OS X is Split View, a subtle tweak that is useful for streamlining the way you use more than one app at a time. Until now, any apps that were maximised to full screen dominated the desktop space individually, making it impossible to work across two side-by-side.

Split View rectifies this, enabling you to choose a pair of supporting apps that will share the current desktop space. Working hand-in-hand with a

revamped Mission Control, Split View can be easily initiated using each app's green maximise button in the top-left corner. Hold this down and a blue overlay toggles the left and right sides of the screen, snapping current and neighbouring apps to the desired areas.

It's a neat trick and one to take for granted once you have mastered it. Read on to discover lots of ways in which splitting your screen can make life easier for you.

Split View in action

We take a quick look at how Split View appears while selecting a second app

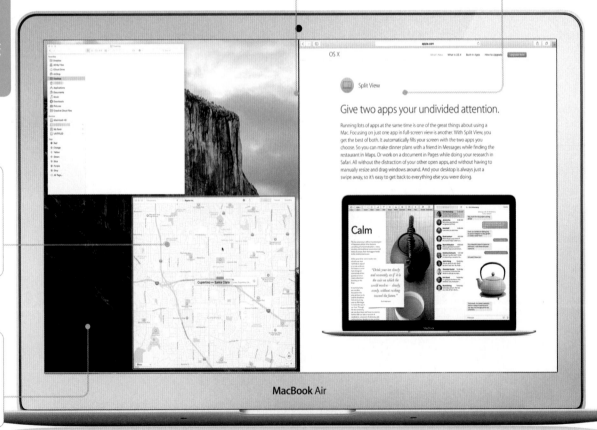

Split View dividing line
When two apps are chosen and both screen halves occupied, you can shift the halfway point. Simply click and drag the thick black line down the middle of the screen left or right to adjust

Things by half
In Split View, apps are maximised within just one side of the current desktop. With only one app selected on either side, clicking again sends it fully full screen instead

SPLIT SPLUTTERING?
If Split View doesn't seem to be working as expected, some users have found a fix worth trying. Open up System Preferences, via the Dock or from the Apple icon, picking the fourth icon from the top row to view Mission Control preferences. From here ensure that the 'Displays have separate Spaces' option is ticked before rebooting and trying to use Split View again.

Available apps
While initiating Split View and with a first app fixed, available apps are shown within the opposite vacant portion. Mouse over and click any of these to maximise alongside the first app, or use the desktop instead to exit

Unsupported apps
Any open and active apps that do not support Split View are shown as thumbnails in the lower corner. Hover over these and Split View will indicate 'Not Available in Full Screen' instead

Split View See in double vision

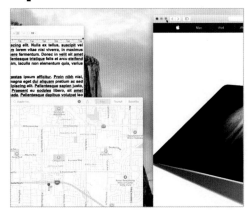

01: Green for full screen

Start with the round green maximise button on your chosen app. All Mac apps have these, the third of three, found within the top-left corner.

02: Click and hold it

Click and hold the green maximise button. If the app supports Split View, the desktop will show a blue overlay below a draggable preview of the app.

03: Game of two halves

If you release the green button without moving the app, it will maximise to fill the current half of the screen, then you can choose a neighbouring app.

04: Switching sides

If you dragged the app to the opposite side of the screen, the blue overlay follows. Releasing the app maximises it to fill that half of the desktop instead.

05: Split or run

After one half screen is filled, you can now click on another app to occupy the other half. Click the first app again to go full screen or the desktop to exit.

06: Split View

With both halves filled, you are now in Split View. Hover to the top of either app and click the green button to exit.

Manipulate Split View

Split View is all about improving workflow and the sense of focus between two apps in a busy desktop. It works in conjunction with Mission Control too, to negotiate windows within multiple workspaces. As we've seen it's easy to access, but also manipulate slightly once initiated. Chiefly you can then adjust the split point from halfway to give one app more screen estate over the other, while very easily dragging each app to swap positions.

01: Adjust the divider

Rather nicely within Split View you aren't forced to use an exact 50-50 split. With two apps side-by-side, hover the mouse over the black divider line. Click this line, hold and drag the divider either left or right to adjust.

02: Swapping sides

In addition, you can very quickly switch the positions of the two apps within Split View. Simply click one app, hold and drag the app across to the other side and watch the two obediently swap places as desired.

Recover files with Time Machine

Your guide to restoring lost and changed files with Apple's built-in backup app

A lot of the files on your Mac will no doubt be quite valuable. There are videos, music, photos, personal and work-related documents, and much more on the disk drive. How would you cope if you lost them? Fortunately, Time Machine aims to solve the problem by making backups – copies – of files, and storing them elsewhere in a safe place. If you lose a file for whatever reason, be it an accidental deletion or a disk fault, then Time Machine lets you recover it.

It is called 'Time Machine' because that's what it is. For all intents and purposes, it effectively allows you to go back in time, and if a folder contained a file last week that you can no longer find, then you simply turn back the clock and retrieve it. It's a brilliant feature, and not just for lost files; you can retrieve earlier versions of files that have changed, too. The latest Time Machine is the best yet, and you no longer need to have a second disk drive in order to use it.

> "You don't need a second disk drive to use Time Machine"

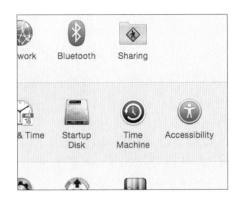

Work with Time Machine

The key parts of Time Machine you need to know

Browse the disk
Time Machine opens the current Finder window or the desktop. You can then navigate the disk, and change to any folder using the usual Finder features. The Sidebar shows Favourite locations

The timeline
On the right is a timeline that stretches from the present back to the distant past. Dates where backups were made to the Mac's disk are in grey, and purple shows backups to a USB disk drive

OS X'S LOCAL BACKUP
Suppose your MacBook at home or work is connected to a USB disk drive in order to enable Time Machine to back up the whole hard disk drive. When you go out with your MacBook, that Time Machine disk is no longer available. Don't worry; since Lion, Time Machine continues to back up files by using spare space on the local internal disk.

Restore the file
You can select a single file or a whole folder of files in the Finder window, and click the big 'Restore' button. Ctrl/right-clicking a file reveals other options, such as 'Get Info'

Back and forth
Guess when your lost file is located by clicking a title bar in the stack, or by clicking the timeline. Then use the forward and back buttons to move one step at a time and find the file

Time Machine Find and restore lost files

01: Turn it on

Go to System Preferences on the Apple menu, and click 'Time Machine'. There is a useful option to show the status in the menu.

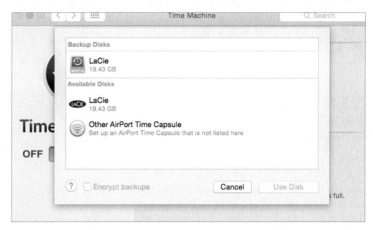

02: Choose a disk

Click the 'Select Disk' button, and the disk drives connected to the Mac are displayed. Time Machine works best if you select a large empty disk.

03: Enter Time Machine

Once set up, you won't notice it. Click the menu bar icon, and there are options to start a backup immediately, or enter Time Machine. Let's enter it.

04: Browse the backups

A stack of Finder windows are displayed, and you can navigate the disk to any folder. Move back in time using the arrows or timeline on the right.

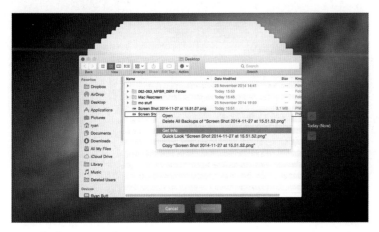

05: Select and restore

A file can be selected in the Finder window, but there are more options available by Ctrl/right-clicking. Alternatively, click on Restore.

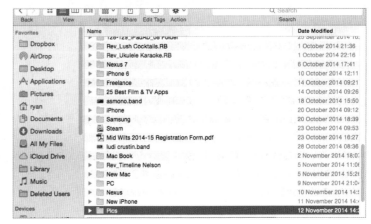

06: Save the file

Time Machine asks you to select a folder in which to put the file. It can be put back in the folder it went missing from, or stored in a different one.

Use Disk Utility to check the health of your hard drive and repair it

Checking and improving the health of your hard drive is easier than you think. With a couple of clicks you can set your mind at rest...

 It can become pretty scary when your Mac starts to show tell-tale signs of wear and tear. As well built as they are, like everything else on the planet, they are susceptible to the pitfalls of ageing. Prolonged use and writing and rewriting of data can cause things to slow down, and in some cases cause errors.

Luckily, Apple has made it very easy for you to check on the health of your hard drive. Using an application called Disk Utility, users can very easily check disks, repair damage and even erase free space to keep the volume healthy and happy. If used on a regular basis you can quite easily keep your hard drive from slowing down and retain that great snappy feeling you had when you first bought your Mac. You will also, with regular use, be able to spot any serious problems before they cause any devastating loss of data.

> "Luckily, Apple has made it easy to check on the health of your hard drive"

Get a snappier drive with Disk Utility

Clearing free space on your drive can have a marked improvement on performance

Erase options
Here you can choose the level of erasing you wish to use. The 35 step is the best, but it will take an incredibly long time. Pick whichever method suits you best

Tab it up
Clicking here will take you to the Erase section. Be extra careful before you click anything here as you could wipe important files

Double check
Be sure that you are making changes to the correct disk. Check and double check before starting actions in Disk Utility

Erase Free Space
This will only erase space that isn't being actively used; so if you've done some house keeping and cleared a lot of files out then this is a good way to get some performance back as a result of the change

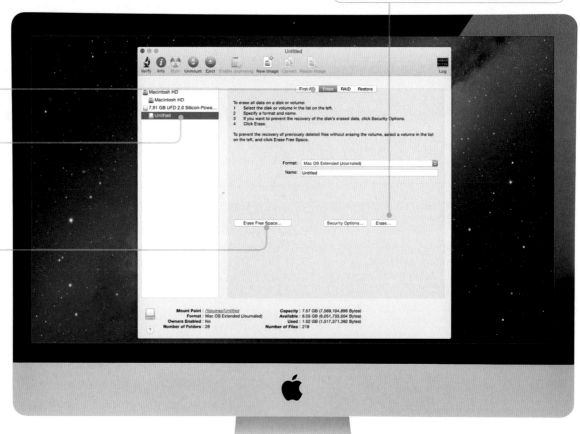

SERIOUS PROBLEMS
Disk Utility may not be able to repair serious problems, but it will definitely let you know if it spots anything untoward. Any serious problems will be highlighted in red and often there will be advice on the best course of action. In serious cases, this will be to contact Apple or a reseller.

Disk Utility Use Disk Utility to repair your hard drive

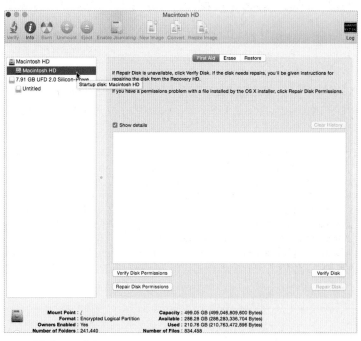

01: Load it

You can find Disk Utility by going to your Applications folder. Once you have navigated here, choose the Utilities folder and double-click on the Disk Utility app. Alternatively, use Launchpad from your Dock and navigate to the folder called 'Other'. You will find Disk Utility in here.

02: Pick a drive

The utility will work on any connected drive, including your startup disk. These will be shown down the left hand side. You just need to remember to click on the disk that you want to check before you start carrying out any specific actions.

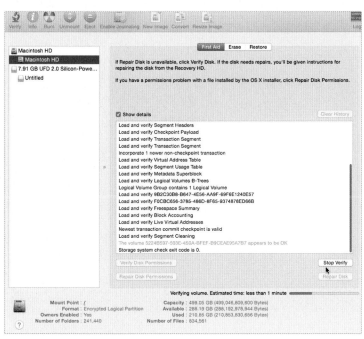

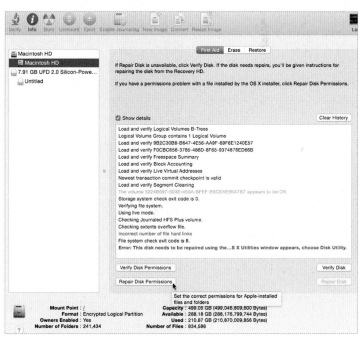

03: Verify Permissions

Click the Verify Permissions button and the utility will begin checking the disk for any errors. Depending on the size of the drive and the speed of your processor, this could take some time so why not go and make yourself a cup of tea while you wait?

04: Repair Permissions

When the disk has been verified you should get a report detailing what it has found. If there are any warnings in there then you will need to click the Repair Permissions button. Again, this could take a while, so be patient. After that you're all done.

Use AirDrop to share files

Get to know AirDrop, one of OS X's most useful features for transferring files fast

Transferring files had, for a long time, been an incredibly tedious process.

Before Wi-Fi was commonplace, users were forced to save their files to floppy disks and USB Flash drives, unplug them, plug into another device, then drag the files onto their desktops. Even now, for many users the process involves creating an email and sending it to themselves, a process that not only takes time, but also inbox space.

Since Lion, there's been a much simpler solution to this problem, and it's called AirDrop. When you open up the finder, you'll notice that there are a number of icons in the sidebar on the left hand side. One of these is the AirDrop icon, which is in

the shape of a radar mast. Clicking this icon will start AirDrop, and any other users who have also opened the AirDrop section will appear in the finder window. From here, you can drag and drop documents, images, movies and more onto the icon and send them through the air quickly and simply in seconds.

"Drag and drop files and send them through the air"

The AirDrop interface

Find your way around the key parts of this sharing service

Scanning
The spinning radar icon shows that AirDrop is constantly scanning for other users while this window is open. They will need to open the AirDrop tab as well if you want to find them locally

WIRELESS NETWORK
Unlike applications like Dropbox and DropCopy, you don't actually need to be connected to a network to use AirDrop and share your files. When you open AirDrop, your computer will start sending out a wireless signal, and when other users do the same, the machines can detect each other. Even if there is no wireless network around you, you can still send files, as your Mac will create a temporary, secure network specifically for the transfer.

Multi-user
If there are a number of computers in the area with a recent edition of OS X installed, you will be able to view them all at once in the same window and drop your files into any one of them instantly

Get Info
If you Ctrl/right-click and select 'Get Info', this window will open. For most applications there is a lot of information, but for AirDrop, all you can really do is copy the icon from the top left corner

Limited options
Again, because AirDrop is a system-level application, you are severely limited by the view options. For most folders you could change almost everything, but this is strictly limited

AirDrop Transfer your files wirelessly

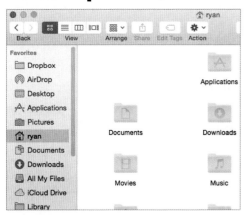

01: Find AirDrop

All you need to do to activate the system is open a Finder window and look in the sidebar. AirDrop is the circular icon with radio mast.

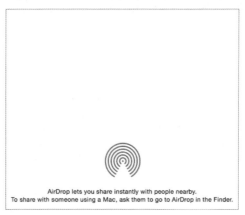

02: Radar on

When you click the AirDrop icon, it will display a radar-style display with a line rotating around the main AirDrop icon.

03: View other users

When another OS X user clicks on AirDrop, they will become visible in your AirDrop window. You can have more than two people at once.

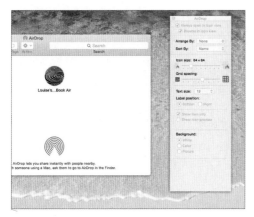

04: View options

If you Ctrl-click in AirDrop and choose 'Show View Options', you'll see a grey Menu. AirDrop is a system app, so you can't change view options.

05: AirDrop

When you have found the file you want to transfer, simply drag and drop it onto the icon of the person who has connected to you.

06: Prompted

Before it is sent, you'll be prompted to ensure this is the file you want to send. It will give you the full rundown of what you are transferring, and where.

07: Receiving the file

On the other machine, a prompt will let you know someone is transferring a file. You have to choose an option before the transfer can begin.

08: Awaiting transfer

As the file is transferring, you will see a progress bar that circles the icon of the sender. It will meet itself at the top when the transfer is complete.

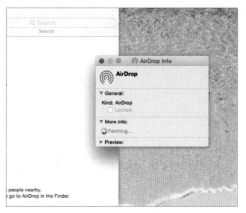

09: Find out more

If you want the AirDrop icon, click in the window and choose 'Get Info' to see this menu. Nothing can be changed about the file, as it's locked.

Set up and explore iCloud Drive

Access your files instantly – anywhere and at any time with one of your Mac's coolest features

 iDisk was Apple's previous virtual disk drive, but with iOS 8 came a reinvention and a new name – iCloud Drive – and a whole host of new features to boot. Not only does iCloud Drive enable you to store any type of file up to 15GB in size, it syncs the documents created in your favourite Apple apps such as Pages and Keynote so they're ready for editing on all of your other Apple devices – just like the Documents in the Cloud functionality.

In this tutorial we're going to walk you through the process of getting iCloud Drive set up and ready to use (don't worry, it's really easy). All you need to do is upgrade your Mac's OS to OS X El Capitan, which is available from the Mac App Store, totally free of charge.

"iCloud Drive syncs your favourite apps"

iCloud Drive Set up and use Apple's newest storage solution

01: Launch iCloud Preferences
Click the Apple logo (top-left). Select System Preferences from the drop-down menu, then click the iCloud icon.

02: Sign in to iCloud
To sign in to iCloud, enter your credentials. If you are signed in, ensure there is a tick in the box next to the iCloud Drive option.

03: Activate iCloud Drive
Place a tick inside the iCloud Drive box. This will activate iCloud Drive for your iCloud account and move existing iCloud documents to the service.

04: Documents in the Cloud
Click 'Options'. Ensure that the apps you were using previously with Documents in the Cloud are ticked. This will move your documents over to iCloud Drive.

05: Access iCloud Drive
Access by launching Finder and selecting iCloud Drive. Create new folders or drag documents from your Mac's hard drive to iCloud for instant access.

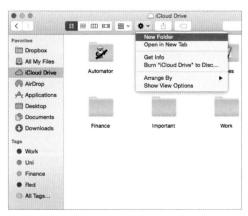

06: Create new folders
To create a new folder, right-click in iCloud Drive and select New Folder from the drop-down. Or, click on the cog icon and choose New Folder.

Create a document

A quick overview of creating and saving straight to iCloud Drive

Launch Pages, Numbers or Keynote
Launch the Pages, Numbers or Keynote app from your Applications folder in Finder. If you don't have them installed on your Mac already, you can purchase or re-download them from the Mac App Store

View document in iCloud
To confirm that your document is being saved in iCloud, select the File menu and hold down the Cmd key. Click on the Save As option – the save location should be listed as iCloud Drive

Set save location
Select iCloud Drive from the left-hand column; alternatively, choose it from the Location drop-down menu in the top centre of the interface. This will be the save location for your new document

Create new document
To create the document, click the New Document button in the bottom-left corner of the interface. Choose a template for your new document and begin working on it in the app as you would usually

ICLOUD DRIVE SYSTEM REQUIREMENTS
iCloud Drive is only available on Macs running OS X Yosemite or higher and iOS devices running iOS 8 or later. If your Mac runs Yosemite but your devices run iOS 7 or earlier, your documents will not sync to all devices. OS X Yosemite is available for free from the Mac App Store, while iOS 8 is free to download on your iOS device.

07: Add items to iCloud
To add items, drag and drop files from your Mac to the folder and they will sync to iCloud Drive – there are no restrictions on the file types you can add.

08: Delete unwanted files
You can delete files from any folder in iCloud Drive – including those for apps such as Pages. To do this, trash the file in the same way you would normally.

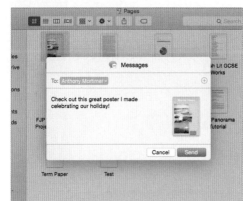

09: Share iCloud Drive files
You can share iCloud files and folders by clicking the item and selecting the Share icon. Choose your sharing method, then enter the recipient's details.

Get to grips with Family Sharing

Get to know AirDrop, one of OS X's most
useful features for transferring files fast

Does your household have more than one Mac? One for you, of course, but also others for partners, children, grandfathers and parents?

With Apple's new Family Sharing option integrated into OS X Yosemite, you are able to link these accounts to one credit or debit card. So when an app is bought on one Mac, it will become available on another and the same goes for iTunes and iBooks purchases. That way, individual Family members don't have to splash out more than once.

You can add up to five family members to your Family Sharing account. Children under 13 can have their own Apple IDs and they can make purchases

using it as long as they have your approval (or not – you can decide on this). You can also allow other adults to grant permission to children within the Family group.

What's more, all members have the option of instantly discovering each other's location. Of course, Family Sharing doesn't purely have to be about real-life families. You could easily set up work or hobby families too.

"Link your accounts to one credit card"

Set up sharing for a child

Have a child under 13? They can
have Apple IDs too

Add the Date of Birth
The Date of Birth is the most important part of the process because it will determine the services that will available to the child and it will also help from retrieving forgotten passwords

WHICH APPS CAN YOU SHARE?
Not all apps can be shared but you can clearly see which can and cannot by heading over to the Mac Store and looking under the Information section on the description page of each app. If it says no next to Family Sharing, the app cannot be shared.

Create an Apple ID
A child can have his or her own Apple ID and this will be usable across Macs and iOS devices. As part of the process, you will be asked to use the CVV number on your credit card to grant parental consent

Sharing your child's location
Want to keep an eye on your child when they are out and about? By sharing the child's location with your Family, their location can be obtained via Messages and Find My Friends

Adding a child
Without an Apple ID, a child will be unable to participate in Family Sharing. You will need to click this '+' icon and then select 'Create an Apple ID for a child who doesn't have an account'

Family Sharing Setting up Family Sharing

01: Open System Preferences
First of all, go to System Preferences and click on the icon for iCloud. To the left of the iCloud window is an option which states Set Up Family. Click on this.

02: Choose an organiser
One person can become the Family organiser. If you want to be the organiser, your credit or debit card will be used by default and you can invite others.

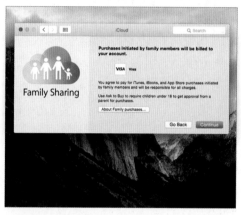

03: Select an account
Verify here to share purchases made with your Apple ID with your Family or select Use a Different Account. Confirm that your payment card is correct.

04: Share your location
A benefit of Family Sharing is allowing other Family members to see your location via Messages and Find My Friends. Just click Share your location.

05: Add Family members
Now you are set up as the Organiser of your family, you can invite up to five people. To do this, click Add Family Member or select the '+' icon.

06: Input a member's details
Enter a family member's name or email or create a new Apple ID for them. The member can enter their password immediately or receive an invitation.

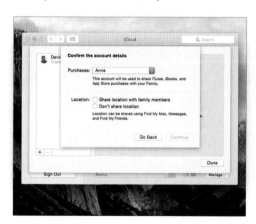

07: Confirm the account
Purchases made by the new Family member will be shareable with other members. The new member can choose whether to share locations or not, too.

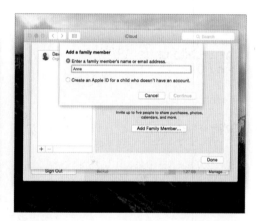

08: Toggle the settings
You can make more amends, like whether individual members can view your location and setting people up with parent and/or guardian status.

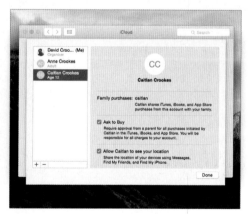

09: Settings for children
If you have a child under 13, you can ensure that their purchases in iTunes, iBooks and the App Store need your approval. Tick Ask to Buy on their profile.

Share to Facebook and Twitter

The latest versions of OS X have social networking options built into their core

The sharing facilities built into El Capitan are more extensive than in previous versions of OS X. In fact, the features that have been added are more like those available on iOS devices like the iPad and iPhone, so you may well be familiar with some of them already. However, while the sharing system is similar to the one used by iOS, it also offers more features than the latter.

One feature with which iOS users will be familiar is the instant sharing of web pages. When you are browsing the web and you come across a page that has something funny, interesting or useful, you might want to share it with your friends. On an iPhone, you'd just click the Share button, and now there is a similar button in the Safari browser on the Mac. Simply click the button in the toolbar and you can

share the page in an email, a tweet or via Messages. The Notes app is a handy place to store all manner of content, such as text, images, web links and more.

It is all synced to your iPhone and iPad, but you might want to share a note's contents with others. A note could contain the outline for a work project or meeting, for instance, and clicking the Share button would enable you to send it to work colleagues. You could share it using Messages if the intended recipients have Macs or

> ## "iOS users will be familiar with the instant sharing of web pages"

Spread the word
Review some simple sharing options

Sharing options
The options available depend on what you are sharing. For example, a photo can be shared through Flickr and Twitter or by using AirDrop

SHARING IN EL CAPITAN
Newer versions of OS X are now more geared towards sharing than ever. Social media sharing is fully integrated into Maps, iBooks and, of course, Safari, which has a new Shared Links sidebar displaying URLs tweeted by friends and contacts.

The Share button
Look for the Share button or icon in apps. This enables you to share the selected item, such as files, web pages, notes, photos, documents and so on

send it by email if they don't. Either way, all the files are included.

The Photo Booth application previously only had the option to email photos and, while this was useful, now there is a Share button that lists lots of great sharing facilities. These include email, Twitter, Messages, Flickr and AirDrop. You can even set your Twitter account picture directly from Photo Booth. It simply makes it more fun to use when you have all these sharing options.

Files can be shared from within Finder and Ctrl/right-clicking any file or folder displays the options available. The menu changes for different file types, so you can share a picture via Flickr but not a document. Finder provides access to AirDrop, which was introduced in Lion and is continued in subsequent versions of OS X. It is an easy way to discover other Mac users nearby and to send and receive files directly via Wi-Fi (without the need to be on the same local network). You just drag and drop to exchange files, so it's super-simple to use.

Finder, Safari, Notes Share files with friends

01: Share with AirDrop
Click Finder in the Dock to open a window and then select AirDrop in the left panel. Do the same on another Mac and you will see each other's computers.

02: Drag and drop
To share via AirDrop, simply drag the file to the other computer in the AirDrop window. Alternatively, click on the share button and choose AirDrop.

Share websites
When you are browsing the web and find an interesting page, share it with everyone by clicking this button and posting it to Twitter, Messages or sending it via email

03: Share a page
The Share button in the Safari toolbar provides access to Twitter, Messages and email. Let's post a message on Twitter about this story on the web.

04: Compose a tweet
A small Twitter window opens with the web page attached to a paperclip. Click in the box, enter the text and click Send. The character count is also visible.

Share your notes
Notes are synced to all iCloud devices, but to share them with another person you can click the Share button and email the note, or use Messages

biscuits

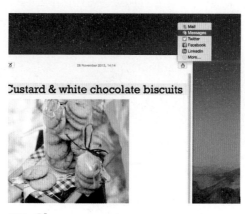

05: Share a note
Start Notes and select one of your notes. At the top of the note display is a Share button that enables you to email it, share it using Messages and more.

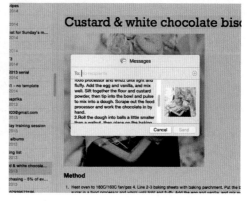

06: Send a message
Select Messages and the note is displayed in a new window. Click the To box and type in a name. Click in the list of suggestions if there are several matches.

Optimise your Mac's memory

Use Memory Clean to purge inactive memory
and speed up productivity

The amount of memory in the Mac has an affect on its performance; the more you have, the better OS X runs. Upgrade the memory if you can, but if not, try a memory manager like Memory Clean. OS X does a great job of managing memory, but under some circumstances, it may be useful to force a clear out using this free app from the Mac App Store. It works by forcing OS X to compress unused memory and reduce the file cache. On the one hand it makes switching to apps in the background slower, but it also frees up a lot of space so you can run a large memory-hungry new app. This may help the Mac to run faster.

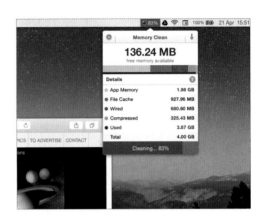

> "OS X does a great job of managing memory, but under some circumstances, it may be useful to force a clear out"

Get to know Memory Clean

A guided tour of the most
important features

Memory display
This is not simply decoration; this bar represents your Mac's memory. Each colour shows each type of memory use and the meaning of each colour is displayed in the list below

Keep tab visible
This setting enables the app to change from a drop-down item on the menu bar to an app that has its own window that can be dragged around the screen and positioned anywhere

Customise the display
The menu bar display can be customised to suit you in two ways. There are Default (short), Long text displays and none. The text size can be large or normal. Set these as you prefer

Clear the memory
Click the Clean Memory button to clear the memory and free up space for running a large app. Clicking it again and even a third time has benefits and more memory is made free

HELP! I'VE NO MEMORY!
Don't panic if Memory Clean reports low free memory. It is just the way OS X works; it's not really out of memory. Unused memory is put to use as a file cache to speed up app switching, but when memory is needed to run apps, OS X releases it. It also compresses rarely used memory, too.

Memory Clean Clear memory, configure your options

01: Check the memory

The amount of free memory is displayed in the menu bar. Click it to open this panel for more detail. The large figure at the top is the important one.

02: Load some apps

As you open app after app, the amount of free memory falls. Click the menu bar item to open the panel and check the amount of memory left.

03: Clear the memory

Click the Clean Memory button at the bottom to boost the amount of free memory. This could be useful if you want to run a very large app.

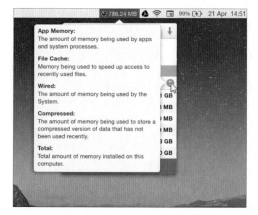

04: Help with memory

Memory in the Mac is used in many different ways. If you find the information in the Memory Clean panel confusing, click the ? button for explanations.

05: Access the menu

Click the gear in the Memory Clean panel or Ctrl-click the menu bar display to access the menu. Ignore the Quit option and click Preferences.

06: Configure the options

The first option automatically starts Memory Clean when the Mac starts. Turn on the third and fourth options to keep the app on the screen.

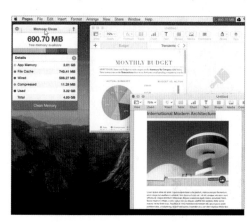

07: Undock Memory Clean

Close Preferences and click the down arrow in Memory Clean's window. Drag it and drop it anywhere you like on the screen.

08: Set Auto Clean

Return to Preferences and select Advanced. Turn on Auto Clean and set the Threshold Level, which is when automatic cleanup is triggered.

09: Triggering a cleanup

When memory dips below the threshold, the memory indicator in the menu bar turns red and this triggers an automatic cleanup.

Understand Apple apps

Discover how to use the essential Apple applications to enhance your lifestyle and boost productivity

"Apple's built-in software is second to none. You'll be amazed at what you can achieve on your Mac without having to install anything extra"

100 App Store sign up

116 Discover Calendar

86 Set up your Mail

92 Browse in Safari

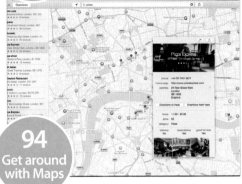

94 Get around with Maps

106
Manage
iTunes

110
Use Apple
Music

114
Check out
iBooks

Set up email on your Mac

Follow these steps to get started and send and receive your emails with ease using the Mail app on the Mac

 It's easy to overlook Mail on the Mac when we're accustomed to browsing emails on the web. And with social networking becoming ever more popular, many people will communicate solely through the likes of Facebook and Twitter. However, if we're lucky enough to own an iMac or MacBook, we really should make use of our sophisticated machines and allow them to do what they do best: make life a whole lot easier! Mail on the Mac is a smart way to manage your emails as you work and play.

Now, the beauty of your Mac is of course its simplicity. But when that simplicity is a new application staring at you expectantly, it can feel a little intimidating. Pushing buttons at random in the hope you will eventually work it out is never going to be the best approach, so with this helpful little guide to setting up Mail on the Mac, we'll have you sending and receiving emails to and from your favourite people in no time. We'll also show you how to customise your messages to give them that personal feel, and explain how to attach documents

and keep the Mail interface clean and tidy so you know where all your messages are.

> "Mail on the Mac is a smart way to manage your emails as you work and play"

Mail Get your mail up and running

01: Run Mail

Click on the Mail icon in your Dock to kick it into motion. After a quick bounce, you should be prompted by a Welcome to Mail pop-up window.

02: Mail's Setup Assistant

This wizard can configure accounts that use the most popular email services, including Gmail and Yahoo. Choose your favourite.

03: Enter your details

Enter the full name, email address and password for your existing email account the same as you would in the browser of your service provider.

04: Create and enjoy

Click on Create in the Mail Setup Assistant and be taken to your new Mail Inbox. You'll have the same mailboxes as in your web browsing version.

05: Compose a message

Hit New Message to summon an email draft. Enter the address of your recipient in the To field and fill in your Subject and message accordingly.

06: Attach a file

To send your recipient a file, click on Attach and pick one. Set up iCloud on your Mac and you can attach files up to 5GB thanks to the MailDrop feature.

Master Mail on your Mac

Everything you need to be able to send and receive emails

Happiness is shortcuts

As Mac users, we love our shortcuts. Ctrl and click on the emails in your Inbox to bring up various time-saving options: Reply, Forward, Mark As Unread, Delete, and Move To folders of your choice

The Mail toolbar

You'll find handy buttons for all the most-used functions right at the top of your Mail interface. Delete, send mail to the Junk folder, Reply, Forward and create New Messages to your heart's content

Keep it tidy

Creating folders to store your emails for quick reference is a great way to prevent oversized Inboxes. Go to Mailbox>New Mailbox and set the Location and enter a Name for your new folder

Sort and search

It's there but it's hiding. Sort by From, Subject or Date Received, and use the Search field in the top right to track messages with specific words in the Entire Message, From, To or Subject

07: Add some style

If you're feeling adventurous, you can change your fonts and add colour by clicking on the appropriate Fonts and Colors buttons.

08: Save or send

If you're not yet ready to send, click Save As Draft and it'll wait in your Drafts folder. When happy, hit Send to start your message on its journey.

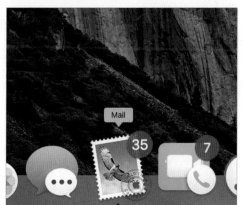

09: You've got mail

Click Get Mail in the top left to download emails. Unread messages are highlighted by blue dots – the icon in your dock also shows new messages.

Master preferences in the Mail app

Increase productivity with a Mail app that's tailored to suit your needs and requirements

Mail is a typically 'Apple' product – sleek and uncluttered, but full of functionality. The latest version borrows from the Mail application found in iOS, and particularly on the iPad. To get the most out of Mail, it's important to understand how to set up and customise it, since this will let you add important things like mail signatures and formatting, control junk mail filtering, and apply rules – which are really useful when you're managing multiple accounts.

The General tab holds a lot of the really important stuff, including how often Mail should automatically check for messages. Accounts lets you control and edit all the different email accounts you own. The Junk Mail option lets you control how Mail filters any mail it suspects to be spam. Check out the preferences to take control.

The Mail interface
Learn your way around the Mail app

Viewing and composing
Control how your emails are viewed, and switch back to the Classic view if you like. You can also set up how a new email behaves when you compose it

Message list
Your email is displayed in a list on the left side of the Mail application, just like on an iPad. The number of messages in a thread is indicated where there is more than one message present

CREATE EVENTS
Mail is able to identify contact details and event details inside messages, such as if someone is suggesting a meeting or sending you their phone number. You are able to click on these and create new contacts in your Address Book or new events in Calendar easily.

Preferences
Preferences is where you can manage all your mail settings. The General tab lets you control automatic mail checking, as well as what sound, if any, is played when new mail arrives

Rules
Rules are great for handling spam or viewing incoming mail from multiple accounts quickly and easily. Set up custom filters to send mail to specific mailboxes without any intervention from you

Mail Master Mail's preferences

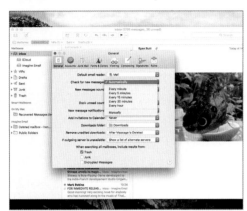

01: The General tab

Open Preferences, and set an interval for Mail to check the server for new messages. Alternatively, you can choose to turn off automatic checking.

02: Manage accounts

In the Accounts tab, you can see all of your email accounts. To manage how each one behaves, click on the Mailbox Behaviors tab.

03: Add an account

To add a new account, go to the accounts list and click on the '+' button. Choose the type of account from the list, or select Other if necessary.

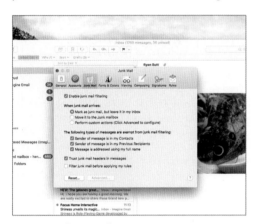

04: Junk mail

Go to the Junk Mail section, where filtering should be enabled. Click Advanced and tell Mail what you want done with any spam mail.

05: Fonts & Colors

In the Fonts & Colors section, you can specify the fonts and type sizes that you want to use. This is handy if you need to increase the size of email text.

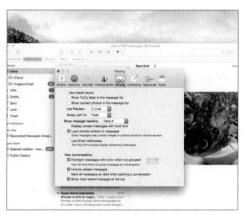

06: Viewing options

In the Viewing section, you can switch between the old and new viewing system. The default settings are good, but you can edit them to taste.

07: Composition options

Here, you can change the format of emails to plain text, as well as disabling spell-checking. You can also set up how replies are formatted.

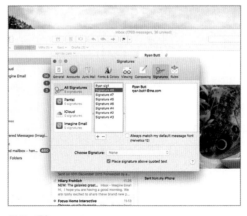

08: Signatures

In the Signatures section, you can add signatures to appear at the end of your emails and choose which ones should be associated with which accounts.

09: Rules

Rules are really useful and can essentially help you to sort mail as soon as it arrives. Use multiple criteria to create advanced rules.

Browse the internet

Apple's Safari web browser makes it easy to surf the web

 Safari is Apple's own web browser and it's tightly integrated into the operating system. Although for most of its previous life it was much more stripped down than other browsers, largely for the sake of speed, it has more recently taken on more features such as Extensions that will enable you to customise it, in addition to a range of things you can change in its preferences.

Perhaps unsurprisingly it is the most Mac-like of any browser – it's sleek, polished and easy to use. Most of its options are accessed through the Preferences section and it is here that you can, for example, change the default search engine and the location for downloaded files.

There are also some great security applications, such as the ability to block the annoying pop-up windows and warnings you get when visiting a website that might be fraudulent. All in all, you'll discover it's a great way to safely browse the web.

"Safari is sleek and easy to use"

Pinned sites
You can now pin your favourite sites to your toolbar. They will refresh in the background to always be available with the most current content

Sidebar
By toggling on the Sidebar you can view bookmarks, Reading List items and see all the shared links from your various social networks

Mute sound
Another new feature introduced with El Capitan is the option to mute all sound in websites by clicking on the speaker icon in the URL/Search bar

Sort extensions
The Extensions tab lets you switch Extensions on and off as well as changing their behaviour

Extensions
Add to Safari's functionality with Extensions…

Extensions are small snippets of code that use HTML5, CSS3 and JavaScript technologies to incorporate quick links to other web services or tools (such as ad blocking) into the browser. The idea is that you only download and install the ones you want and that suit your needs. There are none installed by default. Best of all, Extensions are digitally signed, which means you can't accidentally install malicious ones that might do your Mac harm. They are also sandboxed, which means that even if one crashes it won't take Safari or the Mac OS down with it. They even install easily without the need for you to restart your Mac.

If you head to **extensions.apple. com** you will find a list of all the Extensions available. Some of the most popular include Twitter and eBay, the ability to add items to an Amazon wishlist and the all-important ad blocker that gets rid of embedded ads. There are some really useful ones here.

Key features
What does Safari do that's really cool?

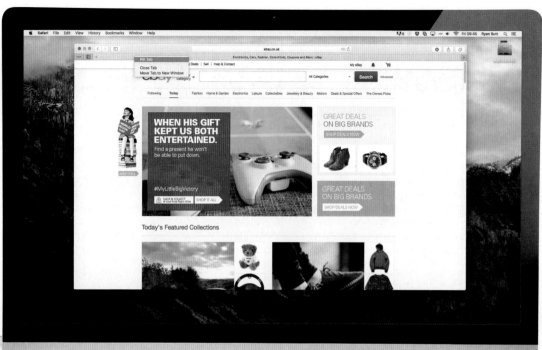

Pin your favourite sites

One of the new features that OS X El Capitan brings to the Safari app is the option to pin your favourite websites to your Safari toolbar. To do this, simply go to a website and then right-click on its tab. The option to 'Pin tab' will appear – select it and the site will be shrunk down to a logo that will appear to the left of the toolbar. The best thing about this feature is that the sites you pin will be refreshed in the background to stay current.

View your favourites

Click the Show Sidebar icon, which is situated at the left of Safari's toolbar. When the sidebar opens after you've selected it, click on the book icon in order to see your Favourite sites, or the spectacles to see your Reading List. The Favourites option saves the URL of the page you're visiting and takes you back to the current version of that webpage, while Reading List saves the content of the page for you to browse offline.

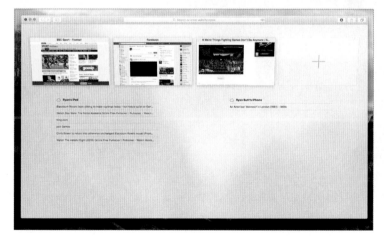

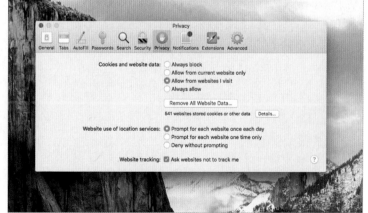

iCloud tabs

One of the best recent additions to Safari is iCloud tabs. Since OS X El Capitan and Apple's latest mobile operating system, iOS 9, work together, as long as you are logged into the same iCloud account on your Mac and on your iOS device then all of the Safari tabs that you have open on one device will be accessible on the other. To access the iCloud tabs in Safari on your Mac, simply click on the tabs button in the top-right corner and then scroll down.

Privacy settings

Online security is very important, and in Safari's Privacy tab there are some handy options available. The 'Remove All' button lets you delete all stored data from websites as well as view this data prior to deletion, and you can also choose to block cookies from certain types of website so that advertisers can't track your browsing habits. There's also the option to control whether websites can use information about your location or not.

Surf with Tab View in Safari

Handling multiple websites is easy using OS X El Capitan's tab feature

El Capitan brings many new features to OS X on the Mac and there are some welcome enhancements to Safari that make browsing easier, more convenient and enjoyable. Along with new sharing options and a brilliant new Search bar that offers results from places like the App Store and iTunes, there is also an all-new tab view that offers you an overview of all your open tabs on one screen.

Tabs are one of the most useful features of modern web browsers. When you are browsing websites and searching for information, instead of going back and forth between sites and pages, or managing multiple windows, you can open them in a new tab. This makes it easier to return if you need to refer to information on them and it enables you to open a group of pages and then read them more easily.

The new Tab View can be accessed using a mouse and keyboard by simply clicking the small icon in the top-right of the screen. Click it and your current page will zoom out, revealing all your tabs in a 3D grid. Tabs are even better when they are used with a Trackpad on a MacBook, or an iMac with a Magic Trackpad. Safari enables you to pinch your fingers together to see the overview with a single gesture. If you own an iPad, you may recognise the tab layout – it's clear that Safari has taken inspiration from iOS 9 in OS X El Capitan

There are several useful actions you can perform with tabs, and if you have an iPhone or iPad you will be able to start browsing the web on one of those devices and then continue on your Mac in Safari. This is because tabs are synchronised across all your computers running Yosemite and devices running iOS 9 through iCloud. This means that you can browse the web anywhere at any time, continuing exactly where you left off if you ever change devices. Even better, iCloud tabs provides live updates between each of your devices. So if you're surfing the web on your iPad, for example, the web page you have open on your iPad will also be displayed on your desktop Mac. Simply scroll down in the tab view to see iCloud tabs.

For now though, fire up Safari, open up a few tabs and grab an input device capable of accepting multii-touch gestures (you'll want one to make the whole experience even better), then we'll take you through the very best of Tab View in Safari.

> "The web page you have open on your iPad will also be displayed on your desktop Mac"

Safari Browse tabs in Safari

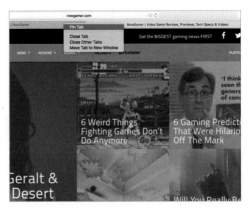

01: Start Safari
When you are browsing the web and you want to open a new page without leaving the current one, press Cmd+T, or click the '+' icon on the right.

02: Handy tab functions
When two or more tabs are open you can drag them left or right to rearrange their order, while Ctrl/right-clicking a tab displays a menu with useful functions.

03: Browse tabs
Click the button in the top-right of the window, or use a pinch gesture on a trackpad and your tab will zoom out to reveal all your open tabs in a 3D grid.

Surf better with Safari

A close look at Safari's Tab View

Fingers or keyboard
You can use two fingers on a trackpad to pinch together and enter the tab view on your Mac. Alternatively, click this button in the top-right of the window

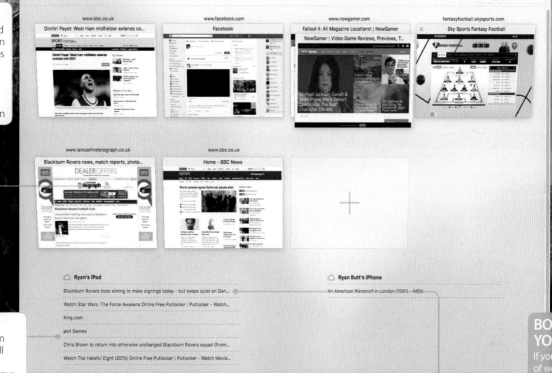

Live tabs
The tabs are live and you can see this icon when browsing tabs that are showing video clips. The video continues to play and page updates can be seen

iCloud tabs
Down at the bottom of the tab view you'll see all the tabs that you have open on your other devices. Click one and it will open instantly

Close iCloud Tabs
Hover over an iCloud Tab and you will see a small 'x' icon appear next to its title. You can click this to close the tab on the relevant device, without even touching it

BOOKMARK YOUR TABS
If you have a favourite set of websites or pages you regularly visit, you can save them all as a single bookmark. Open all the sites on separate tabs and then go to the Bookmarks menu and select Add Bookmarks For These Tabs.

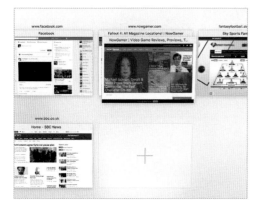

04: Stacking up
If you open multiple tabs from a single root page, the tabs will stack up to save space. You can click any of the tabs in the stack to view it in full-screen.

05: Search tabs
When you're in the tab view, simply start typing and a search bar will appear in the top-right. Safari will search the tabs for the word and show those that match.

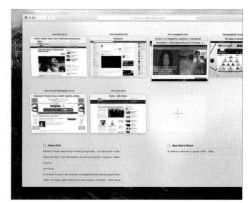

06: Tabs on iOS
Scroll down in Safari's new tab view and you'll see all the tabs that are open on iOS devices like the iPhone and iPad, as long as they're running iOS 9 with iCloud.

Start using Apple Maps

Explore the world, get directions, find attractions, businesses and more

Maps has been on iOS devices for some time and now it's available on Macs too. iPhone and iPad users will find many familiar features, but there are also new ones – and there's lots to discover in this fantastic app. From a large map of the country, you can smoothly zoom in right to your street, or whichever location you are interested in. There are three different views to select from and you can opt to view a standard map, a satellite photo image or a hybrid of the two.

All three are useful and switching from one to the other is very easy and intuitive.

You can find businesses around you or look up the attractions at a place you plan to visit. The information, reviews and collections of photos provided are very useful. If you aren't sure how to get somewhere, Maps can display a list of directions for travel by car or walking. It even displays traffic information and roadworks. There are also stunning 3D views, which are great for exploring cities.

> "There are also stunning 3D views, which are great for exploring cities"

Two views
These two buttons select different views for the map: standard, or satellite

Get directions
Use Maps to get driving or walking directions between two locations

Map icons
Icons on the map show places of interest such as museums, hotels, parks, restaurants and so on

Map pins
Search for places and Maps will put pins on the map. Click one for more information

Shortcuts and gestures

Learn all the tips to better control Maps and get more out of this powerful app

It's true that Maps' basic features are easy to use, but there are advanced features that aren't quite so obvious. For example, Cmd+L positions the map over your current location and zooms in. You can move around either by clicking and dragging with the mouse or using two fingers on the trackpad. Although there is a

zoom in/out control, you can also double-click the mouse to zoom in and Opt-double-click to zoom out. Pinch and spread on a trackpad works too. In fact, there are other useful trackpad features such as using two fingers to rotate the view.

Zoom right in using satellite view, click the 3D button, then click and

hold the mouse over the compass as you push up and down. This tilts the map and, as it flattens, real buildings are displayed in 3D. Many large cities and attractions have 3D views, meaning you can explore London, Paris, New York and other places. Pull down with two fingers on the trackpad to fly over a city in 3D.

Key features
Use 3D views, find businesses, bookmark places and more

Explore in 3D
The 3D views are the most entertaining features of the Maps app, offering a way to explore the world from your desk. Go to San Francisco and see the Golden Gate Bridge, look around the London Eye and Tower Bridge, fly low over Manhattan in New York, explore the skyscrapers from every angle and so on. You'll see world-famous buildings and attractions as if you were really there. There are some amazing views, so enter your destination in the Search box.

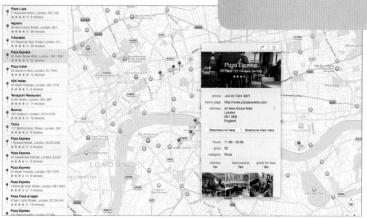

Find local businesses
The Search box in the top middle of the window isn't just for finding cities and streets, it can also track down businesses such as restaurants, plumbers, garages and so on. If you fancy a pizza, for example, just enter 'pizza' into the Search box and pins are automatically placed on the map to show the locations. Clicking a pin displays more information, such as the address and phone number. Sometimes there are reviews and you can even get directions.

Bookmark favourite locations
Places of interest or places you regularly visit can be bookmarked, which enables you to quickly return to a location without having to search for it in Maps. There are a couple of ways to add a bookmark. For instance, after searching for some place, click the pin in the map and then click the Add Bookmark button. You can also place a pin in anywhere using the Drop Pin option on the View menu. Simply click this to add a bookmark.

Build up your contacts
Maps is integrated into other apps and when viewing an address in an email, for example, you can click it to open Maps and view the location. When using Maps and viewing a business or attraction, you can click Add to Contacts to store the name, phone number and address. It's useful to build up your contacts with useful local businesses, particularly when you are planning a trip. You might not have your Mac, but the information is synced to iPhones and iPads.

Find your way with Apple Maps

Maps makes a great route-planner and shows turn-by-turn directions

When you need to plan a long journey and you aren't sure which route to take, the Maps app will provide all the answers. It can work out your current location, which means you only need to enter the destination and click the Directions button to see a complete turn-by-turn breakdown of the route to take. You can also manually enter start and end points, so you could plan several trips before even setting off. With OS X El Capitan, this service has been enhanced with the addition of public transport information. You have the ability to zoom into every turn and see it in detail on the map. Another handy trick is the live traffic information and notifications of road works, closed roads and other problems. You won't always have your Mac with you when travelling, so a great idea is the Send to iOS Device on the Share button. Work out the route on your Mac and then just send it to your iPhone.

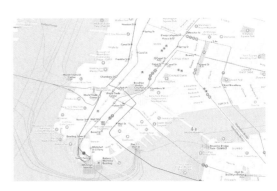

Key route features

Select and explore all the routes

Start and end
After displaying a route, you might want to see the directions to return home. Just click this button to switch the route's start and end locations to find your way

Alternate routes
There are usually different routes shown on the map and each one is indicated by the time in the bubble. Simply select one to see where the route takes you

Walking or driving?
With short routes there is the option of walking, of course. Clicking this button rewrites the route with walking in mind, often taking shortcuts

READING THE TRAFFIC
When live traffic information is showing on the map, you will see roads with orange dots and some with red dots. Orange means that there is heavy traffic, but it's moving slowly. Red dots mean stop-and-start traffic.

Route directions
The route directions are displayed with symbols, but if you aren't sure about a turn, click it to zoom into the map. This way you can step through each turn

Maps Get instant travel directions

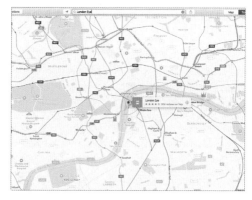

01: Enter your destination

Where do you want to go to? Enter the destination into the Search box and Maps will find it and place a pin to show where it is.

02: Get directions

Click the Directions button to open the panel on the right. Click Directions in it to see the route on the map and turn-by-turn instructions.

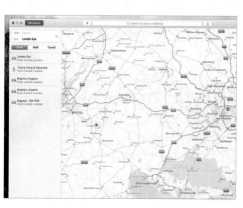

03: A new start

Suppose you want to start from somewhere else. Click Delete Current Location in the Start box and replace it with a new location to see the route.

04: Driving vs walking

This route is a short one and it would be possible to travel on foot. Click the walking icon in the Directions panel on the right to see the path.

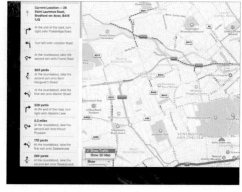

05: Avoid traffic jams

If you are travelling by car, you can see whether there is any traffic by clicking Show in the bottom left of the window. The red roads are the busiest.

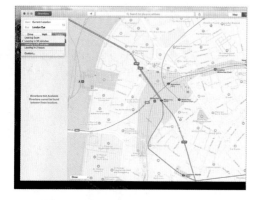

06: Plan a journey

The new 'Transit' view overlays local transport routes on the map and lets you plan your jouney via bus routes and train stations.

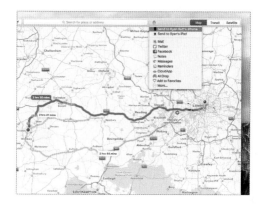

07: Use your iPhone

Travelling with a Mac isn't ideal and iPhones and iPads fit your pocket or bag. Click the Share button and send the route to your iPhone.

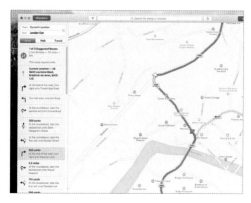

08: Zoom into turns

If you aren't sure about a change in direction, click it in the Directions list on the right and the map will zoom into that location.

09: Switch to 3D

Still not sure about which way to go? Switch to 3D with the second toolbar button to get a better street-level view of the route.

Get to know the Mac App Store

The Mac App Store guarantees easy access to a wide range of free and paid apps. Find out what it's all about right here…

The Mac App Store first appeared in Mac OS X 10.6.6 and is home to a diverse range of apps aimed at enhancing the functionality of a Mac computer. As a bonus, the majority of apps are either reasonably priced or free.

As we have come to expect from Apple, the interface is intuitive, and finding and acquiring apps is a breeze. This is largely because the store has adopted a very similar look, feel and process to shopping to that used by the iTunes App Store. When you want to buy an app, simply enter your iTunes ID and password, and it's purchased. It really is as simple as that. The app is automatically downloaded and installed in the Applications folder, and can be accessed via Launchpad when required. You can even search for apps by title, developer/publisher, category or description. All apps are organised into convenient categories and this makes the process of navigating the store an effortless experience. Here we show you how to explore the virtual aisles…

Purchased
See all the apps that you've downloaded, and determine which are currently relevant

Featured
Browse new and noteworthy apps, or view the staff favourites

Updates
App updates can be accessed and downloaded by clicking the 'Updates' button

Categories
Apps are organised into 21 categories. Finding those you need is effortless

Top Charts
The top apps lists divide into 'Paid', 'Free' and more

Log in to the Mac App Store

Start downloading apps immediately

If you're new to the Mac App Store, there are two ways to launch the service; either click the App Store icon in the Dock, or click the Apple menu and select 'App Store'. Do this, and you are free to browse the store using the 'Featured', 'Categories' or 'Top Charts' windows.

If you've ever used the iTunes App Store then you'll already have an Apple ID so click 'Sign In' from the 'Quick Links' tab to the right of the window, or Store>Sign In from the Mac App Store menu. When the 'Sign In' screen appears, all you have to do is enter your Apple ID and password, and click 'Sign In'.

If you don't have an Apple ID, click the 'Create Apple ID' button on the 'Sign In' screen, and you'll see a window welcoming you to the App Store. Click 'Continue', agree to the terms and conditions and follow the online instructions to create an Apple ID. Once you've completed the process, you can start downloading apps immediately.

Key features

How to navigate the Mac App Store

Featured

Take a look at the Mac App Store's main storefront window. It's well organised, and you'll see five buttons at the top. Select the 'Featured' view, and you can browse apps that Apple has deemed 'New & Noteworthy', which is handy if you want to see the latest apps Apple deems worthy of your time. If you're more interested in apps with favourable user reviews, however, then scroll to the 'What's Hot' section to see all of the top rated apps.

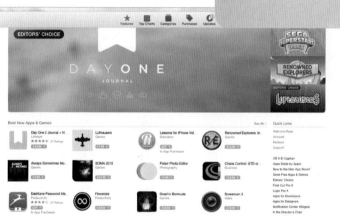

Top Charts

If you're interested in the most popular apps that people have purchased, click the 'Top Charts' button at the top of the main window, and get instant access to the top apps. Here, you can download OS X Yosemite, if you're not already running it, and apps that include Pages, Numbers and Keynote. To the right of the window are links to the categories. Click one, and you'll see a range of popular apps. Each device will have a similar menu available.

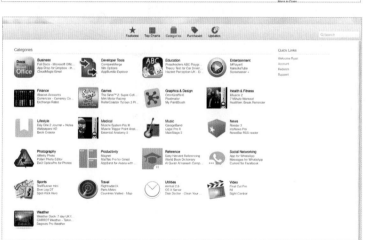

Categories

If you know the type of app that you are looking for, then try using the 'Categories' view. All apps in the Mac App Store are organised into one of 21 categories, ranging from 'Business' and 'Weather', to 'Developer Tools' and 'Video'. Click the category title to see all the apps in that specific category. You can now browse the apps. If you see one you'd like to know more about, then simply click on the thumbnail image.

Updates

The Mac App Store offers similar functionality to the iTunes App Store. If you use an iPhone, you'll know that you are notified of app updates as and when they become available. It's no different with the Mac App Store; click the 'Updates' button, and you'll see all available updates for apps you've downloaded. You are then given the option to install them. These updates may iron out any glitches or add extra features to your apps.

Create a Mac App Store account

Follow our tutorial to create an Apple ID and start
downloading apps from the Mac App Store

An Apple ID lets you personalise your Apple experience. Once you've created one, you can use it to access Apple resources that require you to identify yourself and make purchases from the Apple Online Store, the iTunes Store and the App Store. If you have held a MobileMe account, or use an iPhone, iPad or iPod touch to access the iTunes store, you will already have an Apple ID, and this can be used to sign in to the App Store.

But what if you don't have an Apple ID? Well, you can still browse the Mac App Store, but you cannot download either free or paid apps. Creating an Apple ID is a very straightforward process and, although the majority of people use iTunes to set up their account, you'll be pleased to learn that you can also create an Apple ID via the Mac App Store. Read on, and we'll guide you through the process of creating a new Apple ID for either yourself or a member of your family.

> "An Apple ID lets you personalise
> your Apple experience and access
> Apple's resources"

Access the App Store

How to use your Apple ID to browse
the Mac App Store

Password
Your email address will be your new Apple ID. Type this, and choose a mixed case password of at least eight characters when prompted during the setup process. Use this information to sign in

Sign in
There are two ways to sign in with your new Apple ID. The quickest is to click 'Sign in' under the Quick Links tab. Alternatively, select Store>Sign In from the main App Store menu

Create Apple ID
Enter an Apple ID and password, and you can download and purchase apps. If you haven't got an Apple ID, click the 'Create Apple ID' button to create a new account and personalise your Apple experience

Browse apps
There is a diverse range of apps available for download and purchase from the Mac App Store, but unless you sign in using an Apple ID, all you can do is browse

REDEEM A CODE
Create an Apple ID via the App Store and you are then required to either enter a payment method or redeem a voucher. If you are creating an Apple ID for a younger member of the family, then you may redeem a voucher code. This way, you won't be surprised by any unexpected credit card bills!

Mac App Store Create an Apple ID

01: Create Account

Launch the App Store. From the main Mac App Store menu, choose Store> Create Account. You will now see the 'Welcome to the App Store' window.

02: Terms and conditions

Click 'Continue', and read the terms and conditions. Confirm that you have read and agree to them, and click the 'Agree' button.

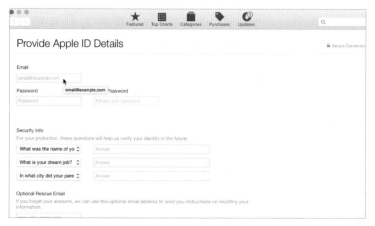

03: Apple ID details

Enter your Apple ID details. Type your email address, a mixed case password of at least eight characters, and the other details requested.

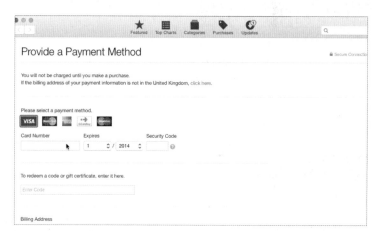

04: Payment method

Click 'Continue', and provide a payment method on the window that appears, or opt to redeem a gift certificate or prepaid iTunes Gift Card.

05: Create Apple ID

Enter your name, address and telephone number, then click 'Create Apple ID'. A verification email will now be sent to the email address you provided.

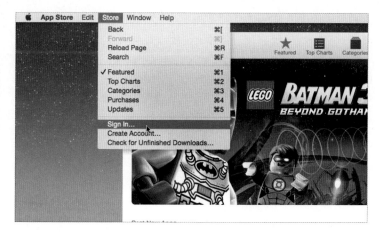

06: Verify email address

Check your inbox, and click the link to verify your email address. You can now use your new Apple ID and password to sign in to the App Store.

Download from the Mac App Store

The Mac App Store is your hub for new software. Here's how to get your hands on amazing apps

When it launched at the beginning of 2011, the Mac App Store offered Mac users an entirely new way to browse and download apps that had never been seen before. There was widespread shock at Apple's decision to do this because it was a move based on the success of the iPhone App Store, and one not guaranteed to work on the Mac platform. As has been the case for many a year now, Apple was right and the Mac App Store became an instant success.

These days, a lot of people take the Store for granted, while others don't even know it exists and have never even opened it up. If this is you, you're missing out on a huge amount of incredible content. In this tutorial, we'll start you at the basic level. If you have an Apple ID, which you would use to buy iPhone and iPad apps as well as songs and movies in the iTunes Store, you can use that to log in. If not, check out the tutorial on the previous two pages.

Mac App Store Start downloading now

01: Apple ID
Open the Mac App Store and look at the Quick Links on the right. Click Sign In. Input your Apple ID and password, or create one if you don't have one.

02: Categories
Below the Sign In button you will see a drop-down box that says All Categories. Click it and you can quickly navigate between categories in the Store.

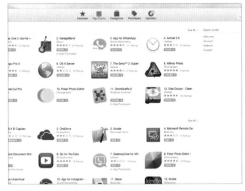

03: Chart topping
Along the top of the Store are five options. The second one is Top Charts; select this and you can see what is being downloaded the most.

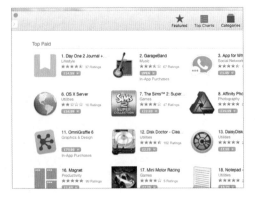

04: Well paid
The opening page of the Top Charts section shows you the most downloaded apps. When you find an app you're interested in, click its name or icon.

05: App details
Clicking on an app's name will take you to its page. You can read a description here. Click on More to reveal all the information about the app.

06: Screenshots
Scroll down and you can flick through screenshots of the app, just like on the iOS App Store. This gives you a better idea of how the app will work.

Mac App Store interface explained

Discover a world of great software

Quick buy

If you know you want an app, you don't have to view the app's page before you download. These grey buttons act as 'Buy' buttons, so you can click these and download apps straight from this page

Past purchases

The Mac App Store recognises when you buy something with an Apple ID. You can click the Purchases tab at the top to view all of your previously downloaded apps

DON'T HAVE THE STORE?

It might be that you don't see the Mac App Store anywhere on your machine. If you are running a version of OS X from Lion onwards, the Store will be included automatically. However, before Lion, the Store was only available on OS X 10.6.6 – Snow Leopard. Earlier systems don't support the Store, and Leopard users will need to download it from Apple's website.

MacBook Air

Up-to-date

When one of your apps needs updating to a newer version, the Mac App Store will show an alert in your Dock. Click it and choose Updates from the top of the window to download the latest version of the app

Search and download

If you know exactly what you're looking for and need to find it fast, you can use the Search bar in the top right of the window. This will offer suggestions of apps as you type, so you can find things instantly

07: Tough crowd

Move further down and you can read reviews from other users. These offer brilliant and real opinions on the app, away from the marketing blurb.

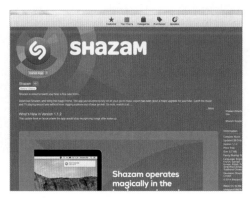

08: Ready to buy

If you want the app, go to the top of the page and click the Buy App button. It will turn green. Click it again, then input your Apple ID and password.

09: Installed

Once you've clicked Buy App, the Mac's Launchpad will open automatically and your app will appear on the grid. You can now click on it to launch it.

Delete and reinstall apps on your Mac

Deleting apps downloaded from the Mac App Store is a breeze

Uninstalling apps has always been a whole lot easier on a Mac than on a Windows PC, and you'll be pleased to learn that the most recent versions of OS X make the process even easier. Don't go looking for an 'Uninstall Programs' setting, as you won't find one! The latest versions of the OS have adopted the automated click-and-hold method used by devices such as the iPhone and iPad. This means that deleting any apps downloaded from the Mac App Store is an absolute breeze. In fact, if you've ever

used an iOS device such as an iPhone to remove apps downloaded from the iTunes App Store, then you'll instantly feel familiar with the process.

Read on and we'll show you how to use Launchpad to delete an app that has been downloaded from the Mac App Store. We'll then show you how to reinstall the app should you ever require it again in the future. As a bonus, you don't even need to empty the Trash, as Launchpad handles everything for you. It's an extremely simple process and we show you how to do it.

Delete with ease
A quick look at the app deleting process

Navigate Launchpad
All apps (paid and free) that you download from the Mac App Store can be viewed on Launchpad. If there is more than one page of shortcut icons, use your mouse to swipe through the screens

Confirm deletion
Removing an app that is no longer required is a breeze; simply click on the black 'X' badge, and then 'Delete' when asked to confirm that you want to delete the app. The whole process is automated

Reinstall apps
You can reinstall apps downloaded from the Mac App Store using the Purchased view. Click 'Install', and the app will be reinstalled, and appear in the first available space on the Launchpad screen

Click and hold
Click and hold on an app that you wish to delete, and all the app icons will start wiggling. Apps that can be deleted (that is, those downloaded from the Mac App Store) will sport a circular black 'X' badge

DELETE FROM FINDER
Experienced Mac OS X users may have noted that apps downloaded from the Mac App Store cannot be moved to Trash from the Applications folder. Although the easiest way to delete apps is via Launchpad, there is an alternative method. Open Finder, click Go>Applications, and select an app. Press Command+Delete, enter your password when prompted, and the app will be moved to the Trash.

Mac App Store Uninstall and reinstall apps

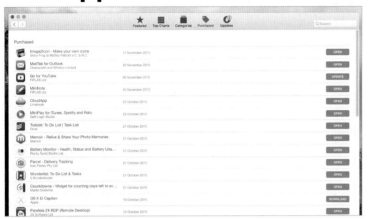

01: Purchased apps

The first step is to check which apps you have downloaded. To do this, launch the App Store, and click the 'Purchases' button at the top.

02: Click and hold

Browse the apps installed, find one you no longer need, and click the Launchpad icon. Click and hold on the app's icon until it starts wiggling.

03: Confirm deletion

All downloaded apps will now sport an 'X' icon. Click the relevant 'X' icon, and when asked to confirm that you want to delete the app, click 'Delete'.

04: Familiar process

The app will now be removed. The process will be familiar to anyone who has used an iDevice, as the tap and hold method is used by all iOS devices.

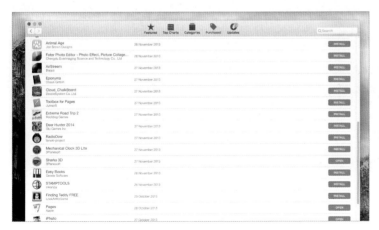

05: Reinstall the app

If you want to reinstall the app, launch the App Store, and navigate to the 'Purchased' view. When the store recalls your purchases, click 'Install'.

06: Track progress

Launchpad will appear. You can track the progress of the app download and reinstallation. The process is automated, with no user input required.

Get started with iTunes

Learn to find your way around the iTunes app and discover all the amazing content on offer

iTunes is the place you go to for entertainment on your Mac, whatever it is you fancy doing. Movies and TV series, new songs and albums, smart playlists that are based on tracks you like, books that you can start reading on your Mac and carry on reading on your iPad, even a digital store full of educational courses, plus podcasts and apps for your iOS devices; iTunes has it all. While the App Store (with its own blue and white icon in your Applications folder) is the place you go to find apps like iPhoto, Pages and Numbers. iTunes is for everything else.

The app comes in two, very big, halves: the Library and the iTunes Store. The front page of the Store has a carousel that you can browse, featuring new and noteworthy apps, albums, films and deals. All you need to do to get going is sign in with your iTunes account.

Once you've loaded iTunes up with your favourites content, you can use the Library, and the iTunes Player, to enjoy your media. Stream through AirPlay devices and sync everything with your iPhone and iPad so you can enjoy it on those too. There's a lot to see, so we'll show you around first.

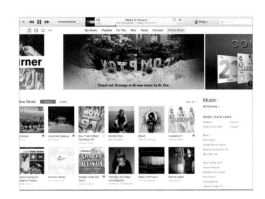

Use iTunes to play media

Listen to songs without even leaving the Store

Access a device
When your iOS device is plugged in, you will be able to access its page of options, including syncing, or eject the device by clicking this button

Visit the Store
This contains a link to the iTunes Store, where you can rent or purchase more content, and you can also have links to things such as your Purchased apps

Find your content
All the music, movies, TV shows, podcasts, audiobooks and apps you own can be accessed via the buttons here. Click on the three-dot icon to access more of your content

Playing files
Once you've selected and played a track or playlist from the main area below, use these playback controls so you can pause and skip tracks while browsing iTunes

STORE, LIBRARY AND PLAYER
iTunes comes in two halves: a Store, where you can buy and rent films and TV episodes, apps, music and more, and then a Library and media player where you can enjoy all this content. While in each, you can use the tabs at the top of the screen to access other places.

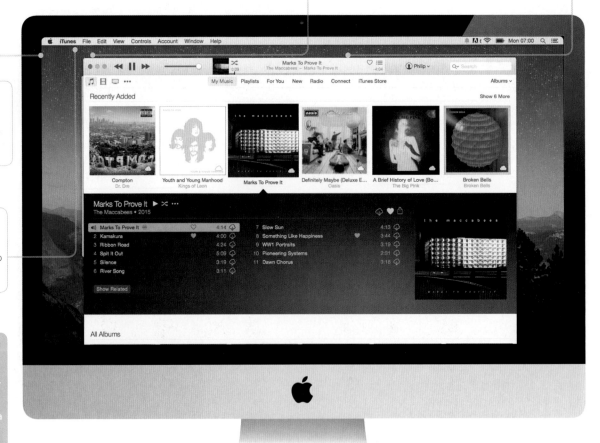

iTunes Find your feet in iTunes

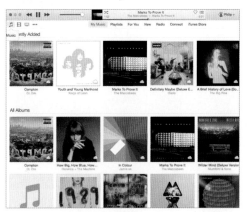

01: Find your music

Open up iTunes and use the icons in the top-left corner to switch between Music, Movies, TV Shows and more. Start off by selecting Music.

02: Browse the tabs

Use the tabs in the middle of the bar along the top of the main window to switch between My Music, Playlists, Match and the iTunes Store.

03: Use the MiniPlayer

You can create a smaller version of the iTunes player by selecting MiniPlayer from the Window menu at the top. It's more powerful than you think.

04: Switch on Genius

Choose Genius from the Store menu to get instant recommendations and playlists depending on the tracks you choose.

05: Match your collection

If you sign up for an iTunes Match subscription, you can upload all your music to the cloud and enjoy it on all your devices.

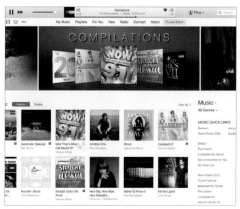

06: Go to the Store

Click the iTunes Store button at the top. Find new apps, music, videos, books and more. Featured content is on the carousel on the main page.

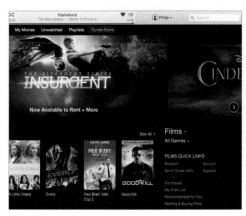

07: Find a movie

Choose Movies from the menu to the right of the main window. As well as featured content, there are further categories. Pick a film you want to see.

08: Rent or buy

On the film's info page, depending on availability, you can buy or rent in standard or HD. With albums you can buy songs or whole albums.

09: Hit play

Once you've downloaded something, it'll turn up in your Library view. Hit play and enjoy it on your Mac, or go and see what else is in the Store.

Download music from the iTunes store

Make the most of the huge catalogue of music available on iTunes

iTunes was born to help people manage their digital music, and over time it has grown to offer all of the entertainment you could possibly want to carry with you. The iTunes library is huge, and all of the major new releases are available to download as quickly as they are on competing services. It has reached the point where almost every artist you like will have a large selection of content on offer.

You can quickly search for individual songs, albums and tracks via the search bar, and also dig down deeper within an artist's catalogue. There are multiple ways to browse music, and once you have an account set up with a valid credit card or gift card code, the process is as simple as choosing what you want and then letting the software do the work for you.

We explain how to download and purchase music from iTunes and then move it to your iPod. Indeed, there are settings you can choose to make the process almost fully automated and with so many options open to you, it is unlikely that you will need to use any other service to get the music you want. Your only problems will be finding the music you require within such a large library and making sure you have enough space to install it all.

"Every artist will have a large selection of content on offer"

iTunes purchasing options

Many purchasing choices are available

Check the popularity
The popularity indicators will give you an idea of how popular a particular track is, which can be useful when making individual track choices

Buy an album
Clicking this button will prompt an immediate purchase of an album. You will need to enter your password, and the process only takes a few seconds. The tracks will then download

THE AMAZON ALTERNATIVE
Amazon offers a huge library of digital music as well, and has built installer software that lets you make purchases, which are then automatically pushed to your iTunes library. The process is very simple, and almost as efficient as using iTunes directly.

Send a gift
Clicking the arrow next to the album price lets you send the album as a gift or add it to a wish list for purchasing later. You can also share the album details with others

Individual tracks
You can purchase individual tracks as well, but if you buy a lot of them it will work out more expensive than buying a whole album in one go

iTunes Purchase albums and tracks from iTunes

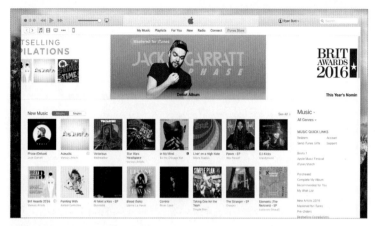

01: The music section

To access the iTunes Store, click on the iTunes Store button at the top of the screen. Now use the side column to the right to ensure Music is selected.

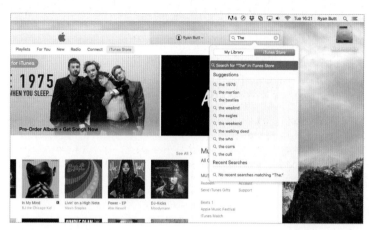

02: Search for music

In the top right you will search a search box. Enter the name of the artist you are looking for and hit Return. A selection of songs, albums and videos will appear.

03: Choose an album

Once you've checked the offerings and decided what to buy, you can click the price button to make your purchase. Individual track prices will be available too.

04: Enter your details

You'll need to enter your password. Once you have done this, a confirmation box will appear. Select 'Buy', and your tracks will download in the background.

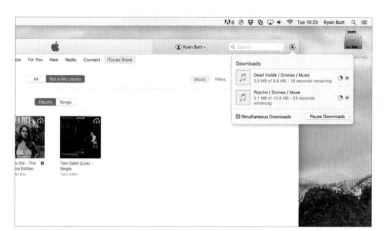

05: Check the progress

You can select the arrow icon in the top right to display the downloads as they progress. They usually download in minutes, depending on your connection.

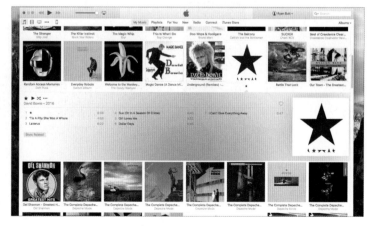

06: Use your purchase

Tap the 'My Music' option at the top of the screen, and you will see your recent purchases. You can now play it or move it to your iPhone/iPod/iPad.

Set up and use Apple Music

Make use of your free, three-month trial and get to know Apple Music

Apple Music is Apple's brand new music streaming service. This is Apple's equivalent to Spotify and it lives on your Mac in the iTunes app. Apple Music gives you access to virtually the whole of the iTunes library (that's a staggering 30 million tracks in case you were wondering) and a 24/7 radio station called Beats One. You can also find out what your favourite artists are up to in Connect, Apple Music's dedicated social network. Apple Music gets more powerful the more you use it, and the For You tab gives you personalised playlists to enjoy. You can

also download tracks and whole albums to your Mac to listen to even when you're not connected to the internet.

Apple has priced Apple Music competitively, so much so that every user gets a free, three-month trial to the service. After that you get the chance to continue using Apple Music for a monthly fee of £9.99/$9.99. You can upgrade that subscription to £14.99/$14.99 and get access for a family of up to six users. So if you're a big music lover, follow this tutorial to sign up to Apple Music and see if you like what's on offer.

"You can download tracks to your Mac for offline listening"

Inside Apple Music

Get to know what's what in Apple's new music service

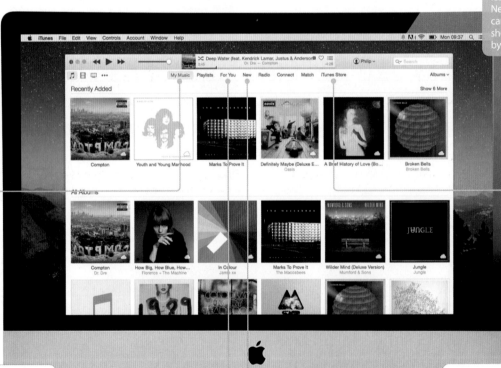

My Music
Any track or album that you add to My Music lives in this tab. It's just like iTunes, with cover art presented in big square thumbnails. Click on a thumbnail to start playing its contents

iTunes Store
If you still like the idea of owning your music, you can head to the iTunes Store as normal and buy tracks, albums and videos just like you always have

For You
When you've told Apple Music the genres of music you like to listen to and your favourite artists, the For You tab will be populated with a personalised playlist of music

New
Because Apple Music has access to such a huge library, new content is added to the service every week. Go to the New tab at the top to see what's just been released

LISTEN TO THE RADIO
Apple Music comes with its very own radio station, Beats One, hosted by world-leading DJs in Los Angeles, New York and London. You can listen live, to previous shows or even to stations by genre.

Apple Music Sign up and start streaming music

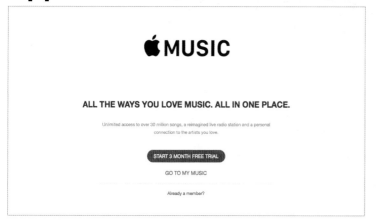

01: Open up Apple Music

Open iTunes and you'll see this Apple Music screen. To get started, click Start 3 Month Free Trial or click Already a member if you have an account already.

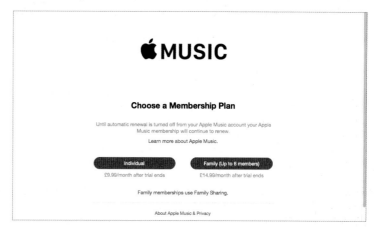

02: Choose your plan

Now it's time to choose your membership plan. Click Individual or Family depending on your preferences. Refer to the intro text to check the pricing.

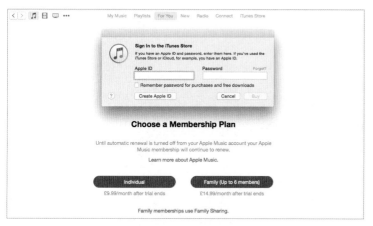

03: Apple ID

You'll need to sign in to the iTunes Store with your Apple ID, so enter your credentials. Click Buy, even though it's a free, three-month trial.

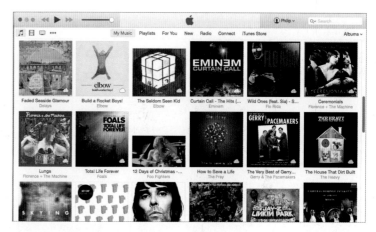

04: iTunes music

Because you sign in to Apple Music with your Apple ID, every track you've previously purchased will be present in the main My Music tab.

05: Play a track

Playing one of your songs or albums is as simple as clicking on the album cover's thumbnail. A track overview will drop down. Now tap the play button.

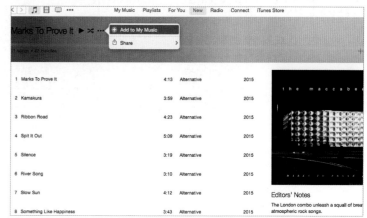

06: Add to My Music

You can search Apple Music for any track or album using the Search bar in the top-right. Click the Add to My Music option to add it to your My Music folder.

Rent and buy movies on iTunes

Get the best new movies on your desktop with iTunes 12

As well as being one of the world's largest digital music hubs, the iTunes Store is also home to great movies and TV programmes from all over the world. To access this incredible selection of brand new and classic films, you can either scroll down on the iTunes Store home page or select 'Films' from the tabs at the top of the screen instead.

As well as being loaded with content, the Film marketplace is an easy place to navigate. In addition to searching through the Store with the search bar, you can also use the drop arrow in the right column to search by genres, like comedy, drama or sci-fi &

fantasy. For some films, there's also the option of iTunes Extras. Not entirely unlike bonus features on a DVD or Blu-ray, Extras gives you the option to check out exclusive behind-the-scenes footage, deleted scenes and much more.

Once you've found the content you're after, you can either buy or rent it. Buying will, of course, be more expensive, but you can watch your film as many times as you wish. Renting, on the other hand, is usually far cheaper, but you only have 30 days in which to start watching it, and then only 48 hours to finish the video from the moment you hit 'Play'.

Thanks to the power of iCloud, you can watch your downloaded film on any device. If you start watching your movie on your desktop computer through iTunes 12, but then have to hop on the bus, you can download it on your iOS device and it'll resume playing from exactly where you left off.

"The marketplace is an easy place to navigate"

The movie page
Find out about your chosen film

TV PROGRAMMES
It's not just films that the iTunes Store offers – you can also download entire TV series or individual episodes. They're not exactly cheap, but you can watch them on any Apple devices you own, including iPod touch and selected iPod nano generations. Most feature both SD and HD options. You can download episodes in the same way you download movies.

Trailer
If you want to see a sample of your film, click on a trailer. You can't download it from iTunes 11, but you will start streaming it when you click it

iTunes Extras
If your film has any bonus footage or deleted scenes, it will carry an iTunes Extras badge. You will not have to pay any more for this added privilege

HD or SD?
Click the HD/SD buttons to change between formats. If you plan on watching on your iPod, it's best to go for SD. On your desktop, we would recommend HD

Ratings & Reviews
Click here to see what other people thought about your chosen film. After you've seen it, you can leave your own review and rate it out of five stars

iTunes Download a film from iTunes

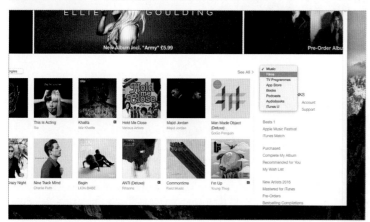

01: Open the store

Open up iTunes on your computer and click the arrow next to the Music option in the right-hand column. Now select Films from the dropdown menu.

02: Find your genre

Click the drop-down arrow next to the 'All Genres' menu option and then pick a genre that appeals to you from the extensive list of options.

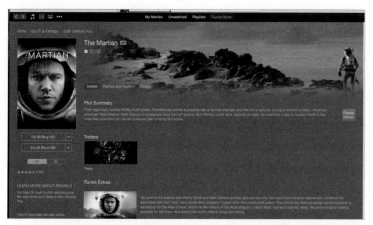

03: Choose your title

Once you've chosen your genre, select the film you want by clicking on it. This will open up the film's iTunes page, which will feature details, ratings and more.

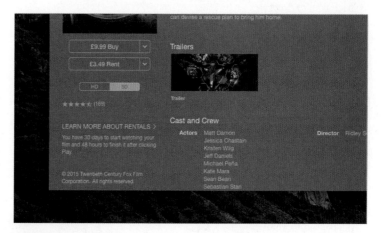

04: HD or SD?

You may have be able to choose a high definition version (HD) or a standard definition version (SD). SD's cheaper, but won't look as good.

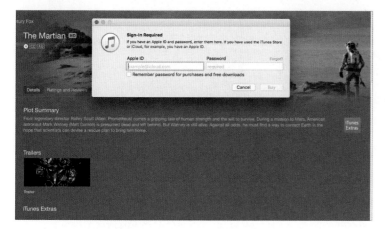

05: Download it

Click either 'Buy' or 'Rent', and you will start downloading the movie. Progress will be shown in the main media bar.

06: Watch it

If you have a fast connection, you will be able to stream it after a few minutes. When it's done you will find it in the 'Movies' section of your iTunes library.

Navigate the new iBooks

Use the iBooks app in OS X to read, manage, purchase and take notes with more than 1.8 million books

iBooks has been around since 2010, first appearing as an app on the iPad. Since then its popularity has kept on growing. iBooks connects to the iBooks Store, which functions just as iTunes does – giving users the ability to have access to a digital library of literature that has made iBooks so successful. Now, with the introduction of Yosemite OS X, iBooks has been made available on the Mac. iBooks syncs perfectly with all your devices, letting you access your books in any format. If you start reading a book on your iPad then come back to it on your Mac, iBooks will let you pick up right where you left off. Although iBooks is much more tablet-friendly than on a desktop, (since you might not be used to reading from your computer) there are a series of functions such as note-taking, highlighting and searching within a book that are so much more simple to execute from a Mac. Follow these six simple steps to getting set up and reading in no time with Yosemite's iBooks app for Mac.

"iBooks syncs perfectly with all your devices, letting you access your books in any format"

iBooks reading interface

Navigating the reading interface and tools of iBooks in OS X

Formatting options
To format a book's settings, click here to access the Appearance window. Here you can change the size of the book's text, choose from a selection of different fonts or change the text colour

Navigation
Here you can search through the entirety of a book with key phrases and words. The toolbar also offers a table of contents and a bookmarking tool to make browsing easier

Managing Notes
Notes can be accessed here by clicking on the page number to be taken to the page where a note was added. Right-click on a note to share it via Facebook, Twitter, Messages or Email

Creating Notes
Select a body of text to open the Notes window where you can highlight text and add notes. From the More menu you can search for the text online have the text spoken

iBOOKS AUTHOR
If reading via iBooks is getting you inspired to write your own novel, then why not download the free iBooks Author software from Apple. This tool lets you create and publish your very own book from scratch or by using templates including images, interactive options and videos – all built to work with iBooks.

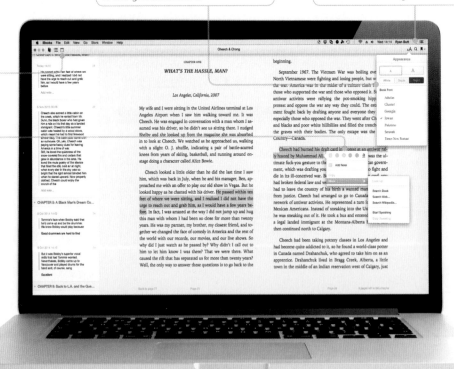

iBooks Master iBooks in El Capitan

01: Launch iBooks

If you're starting iBooks for the first time on your mac, log in via your iTunes account to sync iBooks with your iPad or iPhone app.

02: Build a collection

All previous purchases will sync with the app, placing them in the All Books window. Right-click on a book, then click on New Collection.

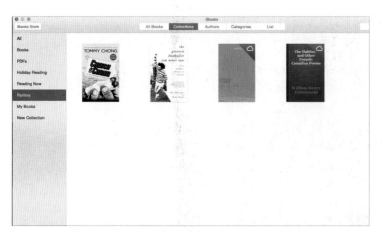

03: Manage your collection

Double-click on New Collection 1 to rename it. Right-click on a book, then select Add to Collection to include it in your new collection.

04: iBooks Store

Click on iBooks Store in the top-right-hand corner. Search by Category, author or keyword as you would in iTunes to find a book.

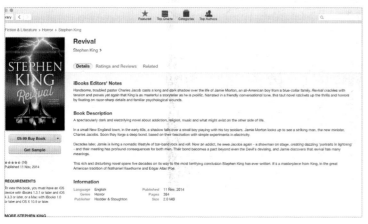

05: Samples and purchasing

Select a book, then click Get Sample to add the first few pages of the book to your library or purchase it using your iTunes account.

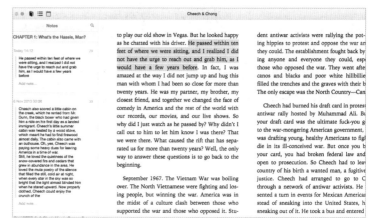

06: iBooks' reading interface

Double-click on a book in your collection to read it. Using the toolbar you can adjust Font Size, add notes, bookmark and search.

Get organised with Calendar

It's an incredibly important app that can help get you organised

MacBook Air

Calendar (formerly known as iCal) is one of the unsung heroes of OS X and iOS. It is the Mac-based predecessor to Calendar on your iPhone or iPad. This application has the ability to really help you organise your life and – with the ability to share your calendars – the lives of others.

As you would expect, Apple has made the app simple yet effective, with an incredibly user-friendly interface. You can colour code certain calendars, for example, so that you can set up different ones for work, social events, sport matches and more. You can set any events that you create to a certain time or to 'all-day', and there are plenty of other options that will suit your needs.

In this introduction to the application, we'll show you how to create a new calendar and add an event, as well as how best to view your busy schedule. Armed with this information, you can keep track of important meetings, birthdays, social events and much more with ease.

> "This app can really help you to organise your life"

Calendar Get to grips with your calendar app

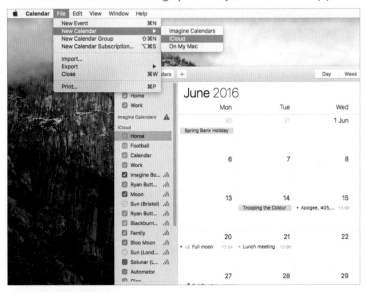

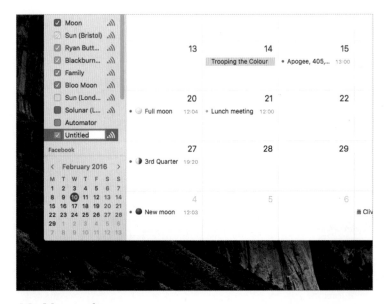

01: Add a calendar

The very first step will be to open up Calendar (or iCal) on your Mac. Use the '+' button in the top left corner of the Calendar interface to add a new quick event. Alternatively, you can click on the File menu and click 'New Calendar' to create a brand new calendar.

02: Name it

Naming your calendar is important, as this will specify the kind of events that you add and help you divide the kinds of tasks you complete in your everyday life, which is important if you have separate calendars for work and home. You can, once your calendar is made, tick and untick it to reveal and hide events.

Grasp the interface

View your calendar however you want to

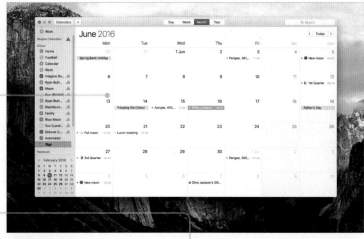

Month view

Use this to view the weeks ahead and to get a feel for how busy you are. You can easily skim through months at a time, which makes it the best place to plan holidays and larger projects

Day view

If you're a really busy bee, this is where you'll need to be to organise every moment of your life. Click on an event to view all of the details to the right

Week view

This is our favourite view, as it offers you enough detail to see entire days well-planned-out, but it also offers a quick overview of the entire week ahead. We live in this view

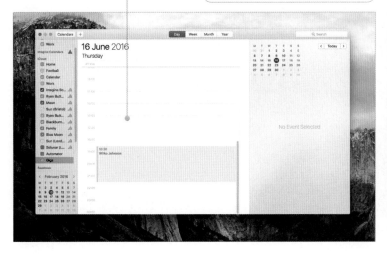

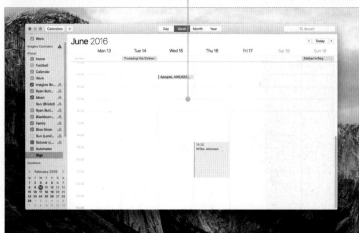

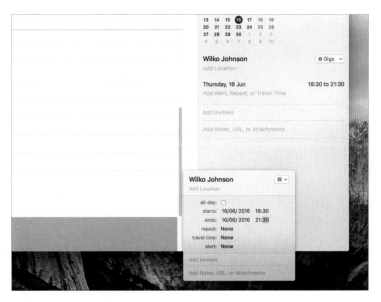

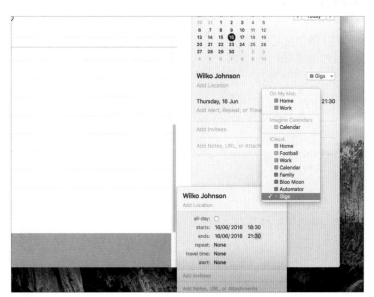

03: Double-click

Double-click on a day and time to add a new event to your calendar. A pop-up window will appear, allowing you to add all the pertinent information you want to the new event. Be as detailed as you can, as this will help you recall the event when the time comes.

04: Assign to a calendar

If you've changed your mind about the calendar that you want this event to apply to, just click on the drop-down arrow next to 'calendar' and select a different one. As these are colour-coded, you can easily distinguish between them. Once you're finished, click Done.

Add a note to a Calendar event

Apply more detail to your events by adding notes

 Apple's Calendar app is great for keeping track of your hectic schedule, adding events and inviting other people to attend them. When creating events that other users will be able to see, it is obviously a good idea to include as much detail as possible. However, you don't want to pepper the main event window with too many words, so what can you do? Easy: add a note. Once you have added an event you can double-click on it to bring up a floating window of information, including the all-important start and finish times, and by clicking the various fields you can then start adding invitees, alerts and notes.

Simply click on 'note' and you'll be able to write as much text as you want into a dialog box and, once you click off the box, this information will be viewable to others clicking on your event. Here's how to start adding in your own event notes.

"Add a note to an event to give as much detail as possible"

Calendar Add more information to your entry

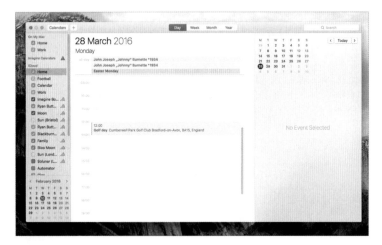

01: Double-click the event

Locate the event that you wish to apply a note to and then double-click on it to bring up an overview box of the event.

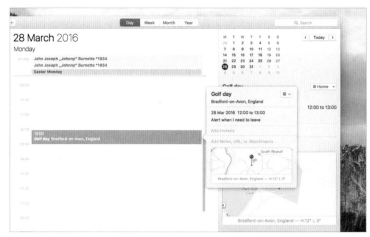

02: Click on note

In the event box will be a couple of 'Add' sections, one of which is Add Notes. Click on this section to start entering your own notes.

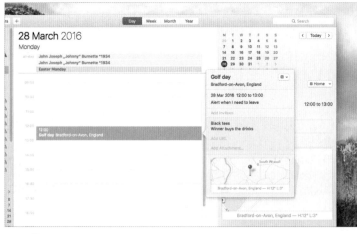

03: Enter text

Type your text into the field provided and then click off the event. The text will automatically be saved and stored with the event.

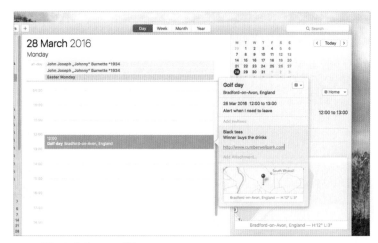

04: Finishing off

There is also the option to add a URL to your event. Simply click on the 'Add URL' field and then type or paste in the required link.

Add an alert to a Calendar event

Set alerts to ensure that you never miss an important event

 For all your good intentions of adding events to your Calendars, they don't mean a thing if you fail to take notice and forget about them. Thankfully, to prevent this happening, you can set yourself handy alerts so that the app will inform you on the day, hours or minutes before or at a precise time and date that you determine. These alerts can consist of a message, a message with a sound, an email sent to yourself, the automatic opening of an application or, if you use AppleScript, you can set up a specific script, or action, that your Mac will perform when it needs to alert you at the specified time.

You have full freedom to determine the time and date of the alert, and you can even set up a sequence of alerts if you're worried about missing your event. Simply use the drop-down menus next to 'alert' in the event edit box.

> "Alerts can inform you of an event minutes, hours or days beforehand"

Calendar Apply alerts to events

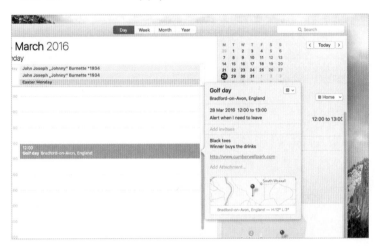

01: Double-click the event
Like before, locate the event that you wish to apply an alert to and double-click on it to bring up an overview box.

02: Click on the alert box
Now click on the time box and this will expand the window to allow you to enter start and end times and more.

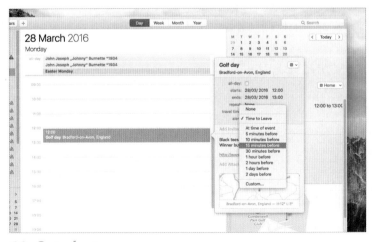

03: Set alert
Set the desired times and then click on the Alert menu. This allows you to set an alert in the run up to the event at a specified time.

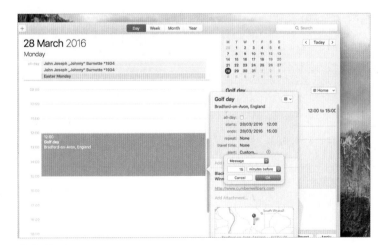

04: Set custom
Click on Custom in the alert menu and then set your own desired alert options. You can also choose to be notified via message, email or more.

Set up Messages for every device

Stay in touch with iOS and OS X users via the Messages app on your Mac, iPhone and iPad

Messages is an instant messaging application that is built into El Capitan, which iPhone, iPad and iPod touch users will find familiar. That is because it is the same messaging facility that is part of iOS. You can chat with your friends and relatives using your Mac as well as your iOS devices. In fact, you can start a conversation on your Mac and then pick up where you left off on your iPhone or iPad because they are automatically kept in sync through iCloud.

The app looks a lot like SMS messaging and at the top you specify who to send the message to. As you start typing, matching contacts are displayed and you can select someone by their email address or

phone number. Down at the bottom of the window is a box in which to enter your message. It's just like sending a text message on a phone, but you can also send images. Ctrl/right-clicking in the message box enables a section of the screen to be copied and then inserted into the message, or you can open a Finder window and drag a file into it. The file will then

"You can chat to several different people at the same time"

Look inside Messages

The new way to enjoy a conversation

The conversation list
This panel on the left shows the people you are currently chatting to. Notice the three dots under one of them. This means that they are typing a response

SMS RELAY
If you are logged into the same iCloud account on your Mac and iOS devices then you can respond to text messages from non-Apple owning friends from different devices other than your iPhone. On your iPhone running iOS 8.1, go to Settings>Messages>Text Message Forwarding and decide which devices will receive text message forwarding. You will then need to enter a code to continue using the service.

appear inside the conversation window. When you receive an image, double-clicking on it opens it in a larger window and there is also the option to quickly open it in Preview.

A conversation is displayed using speech bubbles in the main part of the window and you can chat to several different people at the same time. Double-clicking the person in the left-hand list opens the conversation in a separate window, which is useful when talking to two or more people. You can also continue a conversation later because everything can be remembered.

There are some useful features in Messages, and in the top right corner you'll see a FaceTime icon if the person you're chatting to has it. Click on it and you can start a video call. There is also an option to display a notice when someone has received a message, which is useful when you don't know if they are there, busy doing something or gone. You can even see when they are typing a response.

Start FaceTime
This contact has FaceTime and so clicking this icon will start FaceTime and call them. You can then continue the chat using a video call. It is a useful option to have

Open the photos
This is a thumbnail image showing the photo that has been sent. Clicking on it opens it in a larger window and it can also be opened for viewing or editing in Preview

Type a message
The iMessage box at the bottom is where you type your message. Ctrl/right-click on it or drag a photo to the box from Finder to send it to the person

Messages Get started with Messages

01: Enable Messages
Start Messages and go to Preferences>Accounts. You may have several messaging accounts that can be enabled and used with Messages. Turn them on.

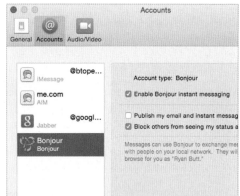

02: Local instant messaging
If you have several Macs, you can select and enable Bonjour instant messaging. This allows Macs to exchange messages and files over a local network.

03: Change your picture
Close Preferences and click Messages>Change my Picture. Click the camera icon to take a photo using the Mac's camera, or click Other to load a photo.

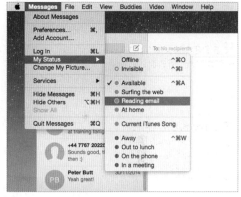

04: Set your status
You can tell people whether you are available or away from your Mac, or even which iTunes song you are listening to. Hit Messages>My Status and select one.

05: Set up iOS
On the iPhone and iPad, go to Settings>Messages. Turn on iMessage. It's useful to enable the Send Read Receipts option to show that messages have arrived.

06: Add email addresses
Tap Send & Receive and you can add the email addresses people can use when they want to contact you. On iPhone they'll be able to use your number.

Discover FaceTime for Mac

With FaceTime for Mac, video calls are now only a few clicks away. Learn how to install and configure this great tool

MacBook Pro

One of the most acclaimed features of the iPhone, iPad and iPod touch devices is also available on your Mac. From the comfort of your laptop or desktop, FaceTime for Mac now makes it possible for you to have a chat or share a smile with your friends and family who also possess an iPhone, iPad, iPod touch or Mac. It is even possible to engage in video calls over your local network. With the simple further requirements of an email address and an Apple ID, a whole new world of enhanced communication is now easily accessible. The sleek, simple and powerful interface of the FaceTime for Mac application is fully integrated into your Mac OS X environment. Plus, if you have an iPhone running iOS 8 or later, you can now even make phone calls to any number if you have your iPhone nearby.

"With your Mac, video calls are just a few clicks away"

FaceTime   Set up and use FaceTime

01: Launch the app

You can launch the FaceTime app by locating and double-clicking on the app icon in your Applications folder or by selecting Launchpad from the Dock and opening it from there. Alternatively, drag the app icon into your Dock to create a handy shortcut if you intend to use the app frequently.

02: Sign in

When the FaceTime app has been launched, you will have to sign in with your Apple ID to start using the app or create a new account, which you can do by opening System Preferences and clicking on iCloud. When you have entered your account details, you will be able to start conducting FaceTime chats.

Find your way around FaceTime

Make calls to your friends and family with ease

Search for Contacts

Click in the Search bar at the top of the left-hand bar and you can type in a name. As soon as you hit the first keys, FaceTime will start making suggestions of who you might mean, and you can call with a click

Contact information

To get more information about a specific contact, click the 'i' icon next to their name. a Contact window will pop up, with all their information from your Contacts app displayed

WHAT IS AN APPLE ID?

An Apple ID is a username and password used to identify you on every Apple service. Whether you want to buy software or a device on the Apple Online Store, music or movies on the iTunes Store or log in to iCloud, an Apple ID provides you with a single set of login credentials.

Audio or Video?

In FaceTime you can now make both Audio and video calls. Click on the two tabs to see your recent calls in each format, and quickly call a person back

Quick calling

You can right-click on the FaceTime icon in the Dock to bring up this contextual menu containing your recent calls. Click on any one of them to call that person back instantly – it's a really fast way to make calls

03: Find a contact

You'll see Video and Audio options at the top of the screen. Click the search bar and type in the name of a friend, or click the '+' button to add one from your Contacts app manually. Then click on the phone or camera icons to make an audio or video call respectively.

04: Make a Call

When your friend has been notified of your FaceTime invitation and accepts the call, they will appear in the main window of the app and you will be visible in a stamp-sized screen in the corner. You can change to Portrait or Landscape orientation by hovering your cursor over the window and clicking the arrow.

Get more out of Preview

One of OS X's staple apps has undergone a recent face-lift. Let's take a closer look…

Preview is a powerful and flexible general purpose utility that is designed for viewing and editing a wide range of different file types. However, it is mainly used for viewing PDFs and images. Since Mountain Lion, it has come with additional features that make it even more useful, such as the button and menus for sharing files. It is possible to share files directly from Preview using Twitter, AirDrop, Messages and so on. Sending a file to a friend or work colleague via Preview has never been easier.

There are now more PDF editing tools and it is also possible to insert pages from other files, as well as images directly from a scanner. Notes can be added throughout a document, but they are hidden. There is a new panel on the left for viewing notes, plus any text you have highlighted too. Preview also supports iCloud and it stores files online so they are available everywhere.

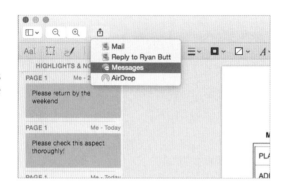

Inside Preview

The best new bits explained

Share the file

The Share button enables you to share images, PDFs and other files with your friends and work colleagues. Click on it and then choose an option, such as Twitter or AirDrop

Highlights and notes

If notes have been added to a document, or text has been highlighted, you can display this panel on the left that contains everything you have added. It is also searchable

Annotating PDFs

Clcking on the Tolls menu and choose Annotate will provide a menu of tools to help you markup and annotate your PDF. These options include adding shapes and more

Markup tools

Click on the View menu and then choose Show Markup Toolbar. You now have tools to hand to add notes, annotations, shapes, signatures and more

PRIVATE iCLOUD STORAGE

Each application that uses iCloud has its own private storage area. You can't see TextEdit's iCloud files in Preview and vice versa. However, Finder shows all files no matter where they are and any file can be accessed using File>Open.

Preview Explore the latest features

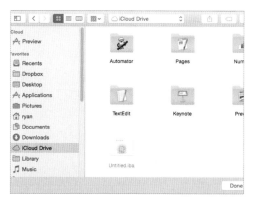

01: iCloud or disk
Start Preview in the Applications folder and select File>Open. You will now be able to navigate to picture files on your Mac or iCloud.

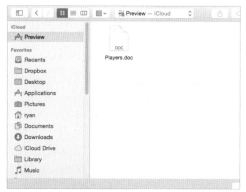

02: Upload files
Files on the Mac's disk drive can be uploaded to iCloud Drive for universal access. Open iCloud Drive and drag them to the Preview folder.

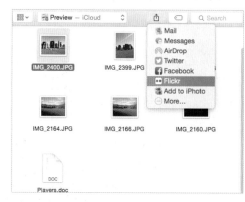

03: Share Preview files
All windows in El Capitan have a share button at the top. Click once on a file and then click on this button to share the file to a range of services.

04: Message your image
Sending files to others is very easy. Here we are sending a photo using Messages. A thumbnail is displayed and you can enter the text.

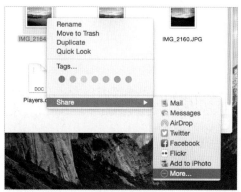

05: File management
There are full management facilities for files stored on iCloud Drive through Preview. Right-click to see options to rename, delete, viewed or shared.

06: Fill in forms
Forms can be created and saved as PDF files, and now you can fill them in using Preview. Open the PDF file and click in the form to enter text.

07: Notes and highlights
Go to Tools>Annotate to edit a PDF document and highlight important text, or even insert notes. Your notes are then hidden, leaving just a discreet icon.

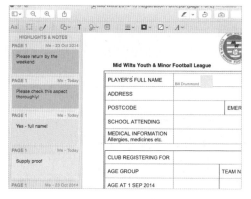

08: View your notes
The sidebar usually displays thumbnail images of the pages, but there is now an option to display all your highlighted text and notes with more information.

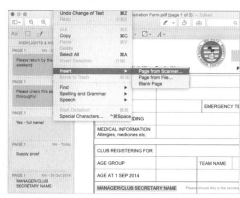

09: Insert a scan
Previously, Preview could only insert blank pages into PDFs, but there are two new options. Now, you can insert from a file or a scanner, too.

Get creative on your Mac

Master the creative facilities of your Apple Mac
to capture and edit your images and video

128 Master iMovie

140 Edit photos

138 Organise photos

"Your Mac will help cater to your creative side"

MacBook Air

"GarageBand allows you to record music, edit and export all with ease"

142
Learn to play guitar

144
Keep time on tracks

146
Stompbox FX

iMovie editing masterclass

Become an expert in recording, editing and sharing video

Thanks to phenomenal advances in technology, you can now record HD video footage on gadgets such as DSLRs, GoPro cameras and even on your iPhone. You also have access to the type of video-editing tools that film-makers in previous decades would have had to spend hundreds of pounds to access. Today the only limitations on sharing high-quality videos are our own imagination and a bit of technical experience.

This iMovie masterclass is designed to help you become more familiar with the video production workflow, so that you can confidently capture high-quality footage, import it into your Mac and then sort out the wheat from the chaff to create a short, slick and watchable programme. As well as overcoming problems such as camera shake and incorrect colours, we'll show you how to enhance your shows with post-production assets like captions, transitions, and a dash of special effects courtesy of green screen compositing and picture-in-picture effects. You'll also be able to add digital camera moves to clips and stills to enhance your programmes, thanks to iMovie's Ken Burns tools. These post-production assets act as 'icing on the cake' and give your programme the type of professional production that people have come to expect.

It's now also much easier to share your footage thanks to social media platforms such as YouTube and Vimeo. Anyone can now find and build an international audience from the comfort of their own Mac thanks to iMovie.

> "Today the only limitation on sharing videos is your imagination"

Import footage into iMovie

How to get your clips safely into an iMovie project

 iMovie keeps all imported clips in a Library. To work with clips more easily you need to set up an event to store them in, and a project to edit them in. Here's how to get clips into iMovie from an attached video camera or a folder located on your Mac.

01: Create a new event
Choose File>New Event. By default the event will be labelled with the current date, but you can re-label it to help identify its contents. Click the big Import Media button.

02: Import footage
From the Import window you can browse to an attached camcorder, external drive or Mac folder. Shift-click to select clips to import. Click the Import Selected button.

03: Create the movie
The clips will appear in the event that you created. Go to File>New Movie. Choose a Theme from the options. Click Create. Label the movie and choose the event you created.

NON-LINEAR EDITING
Once you've created an event, imported your clips and created a movie template, you'll see an empty timeline appear. You can then add your clips to the timeline in any order to start telling a story.

Create a trailer

A trailer is a great way of presenting footage and getting people excited about it

1: Choose a template

Click the New button and click the Trailer icon. Click the Play icon on a trailer's thumbnail to preview its music, pacing and titles. Click Create when you find one you fancy. Add it to an event.

2: Use the Storyboard

Click on the Storyboard tab. This gives you editable text fields and placeholder graphics that suggest the type of shot you might add. Music and transitions are all added automatically.

3: Drag and drop

Modify the text fields to customise the trailer's text and click on your event's clips to drop them one by one into an appropriate placeholder. To see how things are shaping up, tap the spacebar to preview how the trailer looks and sounds.

"You can turn your rambling raw footage into a snappier story"

Enhance your movies

Add titles, transitions, 3D Globes and travel maps

Once you have imported your footage into an event and created a timeline to add the clips to (see previous spread), then you can turn your rambling raw footage into a shorter, snappier story. You can trim clips' durations to make them tighter and, just like editing an essay, you can swap clips around to fine-tune how your story unfolds. Once you have told your tale you can enhance it using iMovie's post-production assets such as titles, transitions and even animated travel maps. The latter are a great way of setting the scene for your latest travelogue.

1: Create some titles

Click the Titles browser (or press Cmd+2). Scrub over a title thumbnail to preview it. Drag the title into the timeline. Edit the font, text and colour in the main viewer. Click the tick.

2: Add terrific transitions

Press Cmd+1 to summon the Transitions editor. This lets you mix or wipe between clips. Drag a transition between two clips. Double-click the transition's icon to edit its duration.

3: Use marvellous maps

Press Cmd+3 to summon Maps & Backgrounds. Drag a map into the timeline. In the main viewer, type in a journey start and end point for an animated arrow on the globe.

4: Add a background

Below the maps are a further collection of still and animated backgrounds. These are great for creating attractive and slick-looking backdrops that can suit any of your projects.

Correct colour in your clips

Adjust colour and contrast to create shots with detail and impact

LESS IS MORE
iMovie's transitions are fun to add, but you can get carried away. Think of transitions as adding salt to a meal. A little will enhance it but too much can spoil it. A pro will use less transitions than a novice.

Balance colour
This icon gives you access to extra colour balance controls such as a White Balance eyedropper. This can banish colour casts by warming up or cooling down a shot in a click

Tweak the temperature
If your shot looks a little too warm, then drag this slider left to cool it down and create more natural-looking skin tones. Drag it right to warm up a cold blue clip

Ungraded footage
Set your camera to neutral for footage with flat contrast and subtle colours. This helps you avoid blowing out highlights and shadow detail and creating over-saturated colours

Boost saturation
If your source clip's colours are a bit drab then drag this slider right to increase the shot's overall saturation. Be careful not to push it too far or you'll create garish unrealistic colours

Increase contrast
By dragging this Shadow Control slider to the left, you can create darker shadows. The Highlight slider will move an equal distance to the right in order to brighten the clip's highlights

Colour correction controls
To access iMovie's tools for correcting colour and tone, add a clip to the timeline and then click here. The Contrast, Saturation and Color Temperature sliders will then appear

Stablise footage

Iron out handheld wobbles for a smoother shot

When filming with a handheld camera, your footage might look a bit wobbly. iMovie can analyse the camera shake and reduce or even remove it entirely (though it will crop your footage after stabilising it). The best way to avoid shake (or a cropped clip) in the first place is to use a tripod.

01: Add a clip
Add a shaky handheld clip to the timeline. Our example clip was filmed in a pool, making it impossible to use a tripod. Click on the Stabilization icon above the viewer window.

02: Smooth it out
Tick the Stabilize Shaky Video box. A little wheel will spin while iMovie analyses each individual frame. When the wheel stops, you should have a less shaky clip.

03: Shake versus crop
Toggle the Stabilize Shaky Video box on and off to see how much of the frame has been cropped. Drag the slider right for a smoother sequence. This will in turn produce a tighter crop.

Speed up or slow down clips

Retime your footage to produce creative results

iMovie makes it easy to speed footage up to produce dazzling time-lapse sequences that show the ebb and flow of people and traffic in a busy city, or slow time down to watch a tree fall to earth. You can even split a clip so that it starts off in real time and then seamlessly slows down during a crucial moment. This variable speed effect is a great technique for enhancing action or sporting subjects, as we'll demonstrate.

01: Split the clip
Scrub forward in the timeline until you get to the moment when you want time to switch to slow motion. Press Command+B to split the clip (or right-click on the clip and choose Split Clip).

02: Adjust the speed
Click to select the section of clip that you want to re-time. Click the Speed icon above the viewer. Set the drop-down menu to the desired speed (such as Slow). Choose a percentage.

03: Fine-tune the speed
After slowing a section down, a tortoise icon will appear in the timeline. You can click on the top right of the re-timed clip and drag left to speed it up or right to slow it down even more.

04: Fast forward
You can also change a selected clip's speed by going to the Modify menu. Here you can slow things down, speed them up and even create a slow Instant Replay of a sporting event.

"You can even split a clip so that it starts off in real time and then seamlessly slows down during a crucial moment"

The Ken Burns effect

Enhance your clips with digital camera moves

iMovie's Ken Burns tools are brilliant features that enable you to add movement to statically framed clips. These moves would be tricky to do in-camera, but in iMovie you can define a start and end size and let the Ken Burns tools zoom and pan between the keyframes smoothly.

01: Click to crop
Add a statically framed clip. This example footage was shot on a locked off tripod so only the people move. Click on the Crop icon above the viewer, then click Ken Burns.

02: Choose and point
Two boxes show the Start and End of the move. Click the End box to make it solid. Drag the corner handles to create a tight crop. Drag inside the box to pan or tilt.

03: Make a move
You can click the arrow icon to swap the size and position of the Start and End boxes. Click the Tick to apply. In this example the camera will zoom in and tilt up as the clip plays.

Use a green screen effect
Combine separate clips into a creative composite sequence

By shooting a subject against a clean green (or blue) card, you can use iMovie's keying tools to replace the colour backdrop. Green screens tend to be popular as many people have blue eyes (and these could become transparent when replacing a blue screen with other footage). This compositing technique is a great way of adding variety and texture to your productions. You can place people in exotic locations or add special effects to your drama productions.

01: Source footage
To get the green (or blue) screen footage to work well the card needs to be evenly lit (or holes can appear). Try and avoid shadows being cast on the card as these might remain solid.

02: Layer the clips
Drag the background footage to the timeline first. Then drag the blue screen clip onto the timeline and place it on a layer above the background clip. The two parallel clips need to run together in sync.

03: Overlay options
Click on the top clip. Click on the Video Overlay settings icon above the viewer. Set the drop-down menu on the left to Green/Blue Screen. The blue card will instantly become transparent and disappear.

04: Reduce fringing
The edges of the top layer's subject may suffer a fringe of colour from the blue or green screen. Combat this by dragging Softness right to soften the edges and reduce the strength of any fringing.

05: Clean up corners
If bits of blue background still appear at the frame's edges, click the Clean-up Borders icon. This enables you to drag the corner handles inwards. Any areas outside the handles will be completely transparent.

06: Erase shadow
Click the eraser Clean-up icon. In our example there's a hint of flower shadow on the blue card at the bottom-right corner. By clicking the eraser on this area we can make the shadow vanish.

Picture-in-Picture
Present two clips at the same time to tell a story creatively

01: Layer two clips
Add a background clip to the timeline and then drag an insert image onto the top layer so both clips run parallel. Click the Video Overlay settings icon. Set the drop-down menu to Picture-in-Picture.

02: Refine composition
Drag the insert picture's corner handles to resize it. Drag inside the picture to re-position. Yellow guides will help you align it with the centre. You can add a border and drop shadow, too.

03: Side-by-side
You can also change the Video Overlay settings to Side-by-Side. This causes the clip on the top layer to slide in from the left or right until it shares half the frame with the clip on the lower layer.

Get creative on your Mac

Fix sound issues
Get your audio sounding its best with these post-production tools

Audio effects
Click here to access extra audio effects that change the sound in more creative ways, such as altering pitch or adding different room ambience effects

GO EXTERNAL
For a professional voiceover, buy an external USB microphone such as the Yeti (www.bluemic.com/yeti/#). This will create a more intimate-sounding voiceover than your Mac's mic.

Reduce background noise
If background noise is competing with your interviewee's voice, tick this box. Drag the adjacent slider to the right to get a balance between reducing the background noise without flattening the voice too much

Pump up the bass
When you reduce background noise, the subject's voice can sound too flat and weak. Bring back some of the lower frequencies by choosing the Bass Boost preset

Adjust levels
A subject's voice should have levels that occasionally peak yellow at the loudest sections. Drag this horizontal volume bar up until the voice clip's sound is strong

Sound fixing tools
Click on this icon to access iMovie's tools for fixing sound. This will summon a handy Noise Reduction slider as well as the Equalizer drop-down menu

Add a soundtrack
Use sound effects, music and voiceovers

Once you've fixed your clips' recorded audio problems, you can now start to augment your programmes with extra assets. iMovie's Sound Effects browser is full of audio assets, from a collection of Foley sound effects to a folder of Jingles that suit a range of programme themes and topics.

01: Add sound effects
In the Content Library panel, click the Sound Effects browser. You can then plunder the Sound Effects and iLife Sound Effects folders for a range of different stock sounds to drag to the timeline.

02: Incorporate a voiceover
Click the Microphone icon to record a voiceover. Use the slider to adjust sound levels before you record so that they peak healthily. Click the Red button and speak.

03: Bring in music
Go to the iLife Sound Effects Jingles folder and drag a track to the timeline. To stop the music from competing with and drowning out the dialogue, simply drag the horizontal volume bar downwards.

Share directly to YouTube

Distribute your programme to the world directly from iMovie

Once you've spent time getting your programme to look and sound as good as it can, you can quickly and easily share your edited masterpiece with a global audience thanks to iMovie's direct link with social media platforms such as YouTube. YouTube enables you to create a personal channel that fans of your work can subscribe to, so there are potentially plenty of people ready to be impressed with your iMovie editing skills.

01: Choose YouTube
Double-click to open up the project that you want to share so that it appears on the timeline. At the top right of the viewer, click on the Share icon. Click on the YouTube icon.

02: Select a size
In the next window, type in some keyword tags so viewers can find your content. Choose an HD size such as HD720p (or the larger HD1080p if you shot in that resolution).

03: Public or private?
Choose a category for your programme and select your desired privacy setting (to make your video public or private). When you're happy, click Next and then click Publish.

04: Publish
A circular progress wheel will appear at the top right, indicating the progress of your upload. Then check out your programme on your YouTube channel and wait for comments.

Share your video to Facebook
Get your work seen on a host of social media outlets

01: Click on share
Facebook is a great place to get instant feedback on your video productions from an audience that knows you. Click the Share icon and choose Facebook.

02: Choose an audience
You'll need to tell iMovie your Facebook login details. In the pop-up window choose a Size – HD720p will be fine. Choose who can view your uploaded movie and then click Next.

03: Side-by-side
In the next window, click Publish. iMovie will notify you when it has uploaded your edited programme to Facebook. Click Visit to see the video on your Facebook wall.

Share with iCloud
Upload your files onto your iCloud for access over the web

Select the movie that you want to share by clicking on it in the Libraries panel. Go to File>Share>File. Choose a resolution and quality setting, then click Next. In the next window, click the drop-down menu and choose iMovie>iCloud. Click Share to upload your movie. A Share Successful message should appear. Log into your iCloud account in a browser and go to iCloud Drive's iMovie folder. You can play your uploaded movies from there.

Get creative on your Mac

Work with external drives to save space

Save precious space on your Mac by storing your iMovie projects on an external hard drive

Video clips will take up much more storage space on your Mac than stills, especially if you shoot at a HD (or UHD) resolution. If your Mac becomes too stuffed with video clips it might start to behave sluggishly, which will be especially annoying if you're trying to edit a video. A sensible (and relatively affordable) solution is to purchase a portable hard drive and store your iMovie assets on that drive, instead of on your Mac. By default iMovie organises its events, projects and

video clips using a library that is stored on your Mac. We'll show you how to set up an additional library on a portable hard drive, so that you can store projects there instead, and how to move existing events from the default library to an external one.

"Purchase a portable hard drive"

Use multiple libraries
Free up some valuable space on your Mac

UHD
HD (High Definition) video clips measure 1,920 pixels wide by 1,080 pixels high. This produces a much larger image than the old UK TV size of 769 x 576. Thanks to advances in technology some devices (such as a GoPro HERO4) can produce video clips at an even larger resolution of 3,840 x 2,160. These huge clips are referred to as Ultra High Definition (UHD) movies.

Add events
Some of the events on the external drive are unique to that particular drive, as we imported them directly to our External iMovie Library from a memory card. Others have been copied to the external drive from our original iMovie Library by dragging and dropping

External library
If you choose File>Open Library>New you can set up an additional iMovie library on an external hard drive. Here the tooltip indicates that this new library is stored on a Seagate Drive that's attached to our Mac

Plug and play
When an external drive is attached, you can access its external iMovie library by going to File>Open Library and browsing to the relevant library. This external library will be unavailable while the drive is ejected

Default iMovie library
By default iMovie stores all of its imported video clips in a self-contained file called iMovie Library.imovielibrary. If you hover over the iMovie Library label a tooltip will pop up telling you where the file is stored

iMovie Save space using external drives

01: Choose a drive
To edit you'll need an external drive that processes video quickly. A drive with a Thunderbolt connection will do the job nicely.

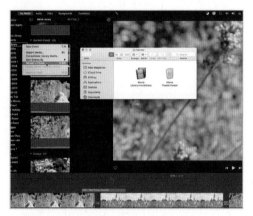

02: Reveal library location
You'll notice an iMovie Library label. Right-click the label, choose Reveal in the pop-up menu. Your iMovie Library is stored in your Mac's Movies folder.

03: Understand the library
Right-click on the iMovie Library.imovielibrary file and choose Show Package Contents. Your imported clips are here, plus details of every iMovie event.

04: Create a new library
Choose File>Open Library>New. In the Save window, go to your external hard drive. Label the new library 'External Library.imovielibrary' and Save.

05: View the new library
Your new External Library will appear in iMovie's Libraries panel. At this stage it will contain no events, projects or video clips.

06: Import clips
Now when you click on the Import Media button, any clips from an attached camera will be imported and stored in the External iMovie Library.

Transfer your events

You can store iMovie Libraries on multiple external hard drives, so you should never run out of space. A USB 3.0- connected Seagate Backup Plus Portable Hard Drive can store a whopping two terabytes of data, and it won't bust your budget at £65. You can also transfer events that are stored on your Mac's default iMovie library onto a library that lives on an external drive, freeing up valuable space.

01: Transfer events between libraries
To copy an old Event from the original library to the new one, drag it to External Library. To move an old Event so that it only exists in the new external library, simply hold the Cmd and drag.

02: Hide or show libraries
You can right-click on an external iMovie library in the Libraries browser and choose Close Library to hide it from video. Then at a later date you can choose File>Open Library and browse to the desired external library.

Keep your Photos library organised

Discover the top ten best ways to keep on top of your packed Photos library on your Mac

Photos is the default app for all your iPhone pics, and chances are you're going to be taking a lot of them thanks to the iPhone's stunning camera. However, the problem with taking so many wonderful shots is that when you want to show them off to your friends and family, it takes an age to trawl through them all and find the one you want.

Luckily Photos has a whole host of features that ensure you are never far away from your favourite photos, and you can sort them in a range of ways to keep your albums fresh and easily located. Here are just some of its options that mean you can snap away to your heart's content without worrying you'll never find that one amazing picture again.

Create albums

Named albums are the best way to remember that special holiday or party. Select a bunch of photos by holding down Command and clicking on individual images, then click on File>New Album and name your album to create a collection of your chosen snaps. It will then appear in the Albums menu at the top of the window.

Last import

This is another neat trick that Photos uses to help you keep track of your pictures. Click on the Albums tab and then on Last Import, which you should see on the top line. This will always keep your most recently added snaps in place for quick and easy location.

Share your photos

One way to keep your photos in check is to share them on social media. Photos makes sharing your pictures very straightforward. Select the chosen photos or album, right-click and hover over Share, then click on your preferred method.

Smart Albums

Smart Albums are a great way to get Photos to do your organising for you, with minimal effort on your part. Tell the app to create an album based on certain criteria, such as photos that you've edited, and it'll do all the legwork for you and stick the completed collection in the Albums folder.

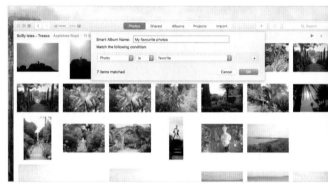

Create new folders

While albums are a good way to organise your photos, sometimes you need a method to organise your albums, too! When in the Albums tab, right-click and choose Add New Folder. Name the folder then simply drag and drop albums into it.

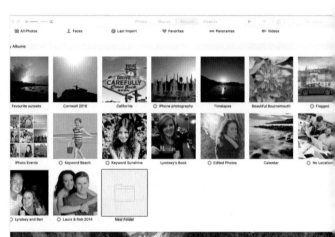

Favourite your photos

If there are certain images in your Photos app you know you're going to want to see again or just love to bits, hover over the photo and tap the little heart that appears in the top-left corner. It will then appear in your Favorites folder.

Inside your albums

Take a tour through the most important tab in your Photos app

Shared photos

Remember which albums you have sent around via iCloud by tapping on the Shared tab. This will help you keep track of who's seen what photos

Little and large

Whether you want to see a load of albums or just a few, you can move the slider here up and down, altering the size of the thumbnail images

Change slideshow themes

Alter how your images are displayed by hitting the Play button at the top of the window and select an alternative style, such as Vintage Prints or Origami to add some individuality

Quick share

Share entire albums with your friends and family in only a couple of clicks by tapping on the Share icon in the top-right corner and choose which method you want to use

AVAILABLE EXTENSIONS

Photos has already started to get some El Capitan upgrades. Image-editing extensions for Mac from MacPhun are already available to users with the latest OS X. These extension upgrades cover the Tonality, Intensify, Snapheal and Noiseless apps and will help you improve your pictures.

Search for photos

Using the same method to tag a photo as to add faces to it, include a description of a place or theme. That way you can use the search bar in the top right-hand corner of the window to quickly locate any photo that happens to include that particular tag.

Export images

As well as sharing your images to keep them in order, it might be worth exporting them to an external hard drive so they are in a portable format. Then, no matter what occurs, you have your albums safely backed up and in order. Hit File>Export then Export photos.

Recognise faces

Just as with Facebook, you can tag people in Photos. All you need to do is double-click on a picture with people in, click the 'i' button in the top right-hand corner and select Add Faces. The app will recognise faces so you can tag them. That information is then added to the Faces album.

Sort it out

Most of the time, the easiest way to keep your albums managed and in check is to sort them in a particular way. To do this, all you need to do is hit View>Sort and select your chosen option. If you know the name of your album, sort by name and scroll to the required letter. Or sort by date if you know roughly when the pictures were taken.

Make precise edits with the Levels tool

Enhance your images using the detailed Levels feature in Photos' editing panel

You're missing out if you have never used the Levels tool in your Mac's Photos app before. Adding the Levels panel to your toolkit gives you some serious control over your images, enabling you to quickly adjust colour casts and light levels from one place, without having to use multiple sliders. The results are absolutely fantastic, especially in photos in which some colours dominate others, and this control can make even the most washed-out image into

something worthy of your wall. And, unlike apps such as Photoshop that offer just three sliders for adjusting levels, Photos has an impressive 12 sliders, giving you much more control over your edits than you could ever imagine.

> "Photos has an impressive 12 sliders"

Photos Adjust Levels to optimise photos

01: Add the option
Before you can edit, add the option to your Adjust panel. Click the Add button at the top, then select Levels from the drop-down menu to have it appear.

02: Use Auto feature
With all of the adjustment options, you can quickly click the Auto button that appears when your cursor is over the section to instantly correct your image.

03: Control black/white points
The sliders at each end of the Levels panel are the black and white point controls. These control the point at which areas become black or white.

04: Modify midtones
The central slider controls the midtones in your image – move it right or left to increase or decrease the brightness of these areas to your liking.

05: Alter highlights/shadows
The other two smaller sliders control the highlights and shadows in the image, or the colours between the midtones and the extremes of light and dark.

06: Change the range
Move the tops of the slider lines to manage the range of adjustment – for example, to adjust the lightest of highlights, move the top handle right.

Stay in control
Master the Levels features with these tips

Histogram view
It is recommended that you add the Histogram to the Adjustments menu to keep an eye on the overall effect that you're having on your shot as you use the Levels control. The Histogram provides more detail

Combining adjustments
Remember that you can still add other adjustments and make other edits to your photos as well as using the Levels control – but we'd recommend that you make Levels a starting point.

AUTO, THEN TWEAK
As with all of the options in the Adjust menu, it is often a good idea to click the Auto button as a starting point to your edit. If you don't like the change, you can always click Edit>Undo to get rid of it, but you can also use it as a basis for your edits and make small adjustments to what the Photos app does automatically.

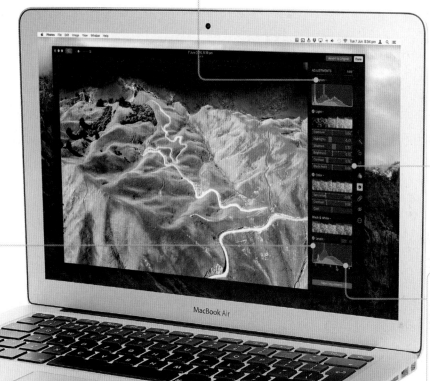

Stay in range
You can use the Range sliders at the top of the Levels panel to select more specific areas of your light range to edit. Drag one over to the left, for example, to have closer control over the darker sections of your image

Fine-tuning
If you want to get fine-tuning control over an adjustment that you've made, hold down the Alt key on your keyboard and drag the bottom slider on the Levels panel. This moves both the top and bottom sliders in unison

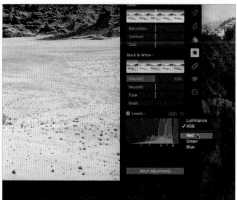

07: Access more options
These changes are only those available in the RGB section. Click the menu button in the Levels panel to change to options like Luminescence.

08: Control colour
If, for example, your image has dominant green tones but lacks punchy red tones, you can select the relevant sections to adjust only these colours.

09: Perfect and save
Once you're happy with the changes you've made with the Levels panel, you can continue editing, or simply click Done to save your shot.

Learn how to play with free lessons

Discover how GarageBand provides guitar and piano tutelage no matter what level

Learning to play an instrument is a rewarding struggle. Most people begin by attempting to master the fundamental techniques before advancing. Aside from merely recording and mixing your compositions, GarageBand acknowledges this vital learning stage by providing exercises for guitar and piano. As part of its Learn to Play feature, the app offers 38 free modules ranging from beginner to more advanced. Budding guitarists can learn basic chord shapes and progressions, while practising pianists can learn classical and pop styles. The Play chapter then invites you to record your progress.

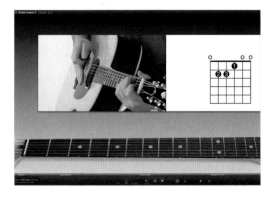

> "GarageBand offers 38 free modules ranging from beginner to advanced"

GarageBand Learn an instrument in GarageBand

01: Finding lessons
Guitar and piano lessons are listed under the Learn to Play tab in the New Project dialog. They appear after being downloaded via the Lesson Store tab.

02: Open a lesson
With lessons downloading or available, simply select the one you wish to open and double-click to begin. The lesson will open and start full screen.

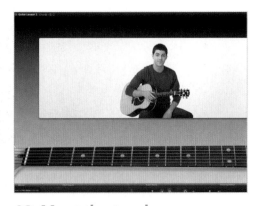

03: Meet the teacher
A teacher who instructs directly from a main window hosts each lesson. You can toggle pause or play, or even skip/scrub forwards and back.

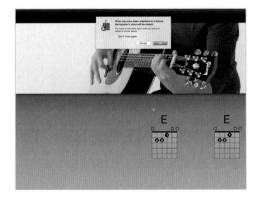

04: Advanced playback
Beyond basic controls, clicking the chapter markers skips progress. Toggle the yellow cycle region via the loop button or slow down playback with the slider.

05: Input monitoring
With guitar or keyboard interfaced, you are invited to play along and monitor output. The light next to the metronome glows red to indicate input signal.

06: Play chapter
Hover over the Teacher pane to switch to the Play chapter. Here you can capture your playing and grade progress with the 'How did I play' feature.

Teacher's pet

Familiarise yourself with the main interface elements and tools

Teacher window

This is the main panel where the teacher addresses you and demonstrates the featured techniques as you follow. Hover over this to switch between Learn and Play chapters, or toggle focal points

ARTIST LESSONS

Another technique favoured by fledgling musicians is to emulate their heroes by learning popular songs. Artist Lessons extend Learn to Play by delivering music stars like Sting, Norah Jones and John Legend as your own personal tutors. Each explains guitar and piano techniques behind playing their most successful hits and must be purchased from within GarageBand.

Lesson menu

This top menu houses a Glossary of technical and musical terminology and a handy tuner for guitar. The Mixer has volume controls for varying the component audio levels, while Setup defines preferences for inputs and lesson behaviours

Instrument and notation

Below the teacher you will find either a guitar neck or set of piano keys – depending on the lesson type – indicating associated finger positions. By default you will automatically see music notation appear above this where required

Chapters and controls

At the bottom of the lesson is a duration bar with chapter markers. Here you'll notice a playhead moves along to denote progress, while below are controls for playback alongside speed and volume sliders

07: Guitar tuner

During guitar lessons, you can access a tuner from the menu in the top right. Here you can click each string to pluck and get tips on fine-tuning.

08: Mixer controls

Pick the Mixer menu option to view sliders for setting the teacher's voice and instrument volume, the band and your own instrument or recordings.

09: Setup options

The Setup options provide controls for choosing instrument inputs and toggling monitoring. Personalised lesson options are also found here.

Keep time with Tempo Track techniques

Tempo is at the heart of GarageBand and these are the crucial tools for making it tick

For new GarageBand users, perhaps the single most important concept to master within GarageBand is tempo. All music projects are built around a predefined global tempo, measured in beats per minute (bpm) and set within the control bar's LCD. Beginning from a fairly typical 120bpm, lowering or increasing the tempo will dramatically dictate the pace of your project, most crucially rhythm loops or Drummer tracks. Importantly though, GarageBand also allows

for the project tempo to be changed mid-song using a Tempo Track and a series of automation points. This is vital for keeping time the way you want for certain passages within broader and more complex compositions.

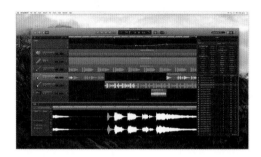

"The tempo is measured in bpm"

Tracking down tempo
The timing tools you'll need to keep the beat flowing

Project tempo display
The current project tempo is measured in beats per minute, with new projects created at 120bpm. It is displayed within the control bar LCD and can be clicked and dragged, or double-clicked to edit the Tempo field

FLEX TIME EDITING
GarageBand implements timing tweaks within audio regions using Flex Time, applying this automatically when groove matching. This can also be toggled on manually by enabling Flex within the Audio Editor inspector. Clicking a peak or 'transient' within the audio waveform adds a flex marker, which can be clicked and dragged to stretch the timing out or compress it – making more precise timing edits.

The Tempo Track
Project tempo changes can be automated throughout a song using the tempo track. This is displayed by choosing Track>Show Tempo Track from the main menu bar and can be expanded out as required

Groove Track
Tracks can have their timing synchronised around a nominated groove track, denoted by the gold star within the header. Subsequent tracks are then told to follow by ticking the Match Groove Track box to the left of each header

Tempo points
Changes are defined within the tempo track by editing points that plot the bpm shifts within an adjustable range. Points can be added, deleted, moved, copied and used to form gradual curves just as you would automations

GarageBand Time-keeping with the Tempo Track

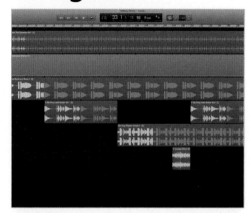

01: Set beats per minute

Projects begin with a tempo, typically set at 120bpm. The tempo is shown and easily changed via the control bar LCD – just click and drag it.

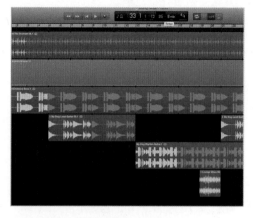

02: Edit overall tempo

Double-click the Tempo count to enter a specific bpm. The change immediately dictates the pace of loops for tracks adhering to overall project tempo.

03: Show Tempo Track

You can use the Tempo Track to slow or speed up the bpm throughout the song. Show it via Track>Show Tempo Track or with Shift+Cmd+T.

04: Plot tempo points

The Tempo Track shows a line for the base-level project tempo. Raise or lower bpm above or below this line by double-clicking the target time position.

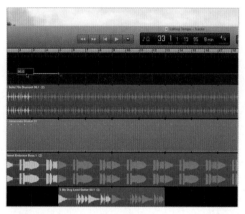

05: Position points

Tempo points are dragged up and down, or you can position them numerically by holding the Ctrl+Alt+Cmd keys when you click the target time.

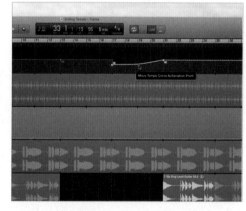

06: Ensure smooth transitions

Make tempo shifts more gradual by dragging the black dot that appears above or below a second point. Click and drag to draw a smooth, curved line.

How to sync track timing

With the tempo set, you may still find that certain tracks are not quite locked in when it comes to timing. This tends to apply more to recorded performance or real instrument tracks where the musician's timing may have strayed slightly for whatever reason. GarageBand helps you counteract this by choosing a Groove Track that subsequent tracks can follow and lock themselves into.

01: Choose the groove

The Groove Track is the constant rhythmic bedrock through a project, such as a bassline. Show it via Track>Track Header>Show Groove Track before hovering over the edge of the selected header and clicking the star to select.

02: Match other tracks

Other tracks are matched to the chosen Groove Track by ticking the boxes situated to the left of each track header. These can be toggled on and off instantly to preview, applying Flex Time markers to the region to affect the change.

Chain and optimise stompbox effects

Master the fundamentals of linking and routing GarageBand's virtual FX pedals

Ah, the electric guitar effects pedal – the stompbox if you will. For guitarists they are the gear equivalent of designer handbags – they can never have too many and it's often the vintage, expensive ones that are the most attractive. Garageband does an awesome job of modelling popular units virtually, emulating the most desirable effects across genre and era. Whether you want to apply fuzz or overdrive distortions, pitch shifters, chorus, delays and even

wah-wah, GarageBand has a pedalboard for chaining stompboxes together. In this guide we'll look at that pedalboard and the core techniques required for arranging multiple units, as well as signal routing for more advanced configurations.

"Apply fuzz or overdrive distortions"

GarageBand Working with guitar stompbox effects

01: Locate Stompbox icon
With a guitar track already in your project, view Smart Controls with the B key and click the small Stompbox button to show the pedalboard.

02: Declutter pedalboard
This floating window will contain any default effect pedals within the selected track's guitar patch. Remove any by dragging them out the main area.

03: Add new effects
New pedals are added to the pedalboard by dragging them into the main space from the browser to the right.

04: Arrange the order
As you add pedals you create a signal 'chain' running from left to right across the board. The order will impact on the final sound.

05: Examine Router panel
Hover the cursor over the grey strip above the pedals, known as the Router. You will see a series of labelled boxes representing each pedal in the chain.

06: Split the signal
Click the first effect box in the Router panel. The chain splits to place the pedal on a different signal 'bus', adding a Mixer control unit onto the end.

Pick out the pedalboard

Navigate GarageBand's pedalboard and identify the main areas of interest

Router panel

The area above the pedals is the Router, which is used to manipulate the signal flow along two effect buses. These are known as Bus A and B, shown as two horizontal path lines with effects occupying either

Pedal browser

This panel shows the available stompboxes that can be clicked and dragged into the pedal area to the left. The selection is filtered by Distortion, Pitch, Modulation, Delay Filter and Utility pedal types via the drop-down menu

WHY ROUTE THE SIGNAL?

By routing a signal between two A and B buses, GarageBand opens up the possibilities in terms of chaining. Instead of sending sound through each unit merely sequentially, splitting and routing the signal runs it in parallel. It then uses a Mixer control to blend that sound back together in stereo, or switch between two very differently effected bus signals.

MacBook Air

Pedal area

This is the largest portion of the pedalboard, expanding to the right as you drag in additional effects from the adjacent browser. Once in, they can be dragged around to reorder or moved outside the area to remove

Mixer/Splitter Controls

Mixer controls the level relationship between buses A and B, how much is heard from each and how they should pan. Similarly, the Splitter controls are also shown when routing the signal according to frequency between buses

07: Join the dots

Effects can be dragged between the two bus lines. You'll see some little junction dots between pedals which toggle where the signal splits.

08: Mix it up

The Mixer control mixes the two bus signals back into one and can move within the pedal chain. Experiment with the A/B switches or the Pan knobs.

09: Split frequencies

Splitter controls can be added between pedals, or wherever an empty split point is found. They evenly split the signal between B and A buses.

Work with your Mac

Learn how to make the most of productivity apps to work smarter – either at home or in the office

150
Understand Notes

152
Manage contacts

"Pages, Numbers and Keynote are all excellent office apps, and should easily cover most of your needs"

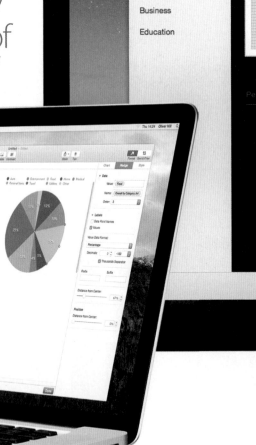

160
Visualise your Numbers data with charts and graphs

154
Learn to use Pages

156
Make a template

162
Use notes in Keynote

Master the many features of Notes

Improve and expand your note-taking options with plenty of great features in the El Capitan version of Notes

Apple has spent a fair bit of time building a new Notes app that has a slightly different design but lots of new features. It is better than ever and certainly much more useful. Among the new features is support for almost every type of file and content you might want to store in a note. For example, you can add photos, videos, audio, maps, web links,

sketches, PDFs and so on. When you click the Share button in an app you now have the option to store the content in a note.

Many apps have sharing facilities and we look at a couple in the step-by-step guide. There are others and it makes it easy for you to build notes and store items that you need for a work or personal project.

"You can add photos, videos, audio, maps, web links, sketches and so on"

A guided tour of what's new

Take advantage of the new features on offer

MacBook Air

SYNCING NOTES
Notes works with iCloud and this means that it is available on other Macs and iOS devices that connect to iCloud. Notes created on one device or computer can be viewed and edited on another. This feature must be turned on in iCloud in System Preferences. Go there and check that it is being used.

Checklists
It might look a bit like a clock, but this is the checklist button – a circle with a tick. Click it to add checklists to notes, such as shopping lists, to-do items or tasks to complete

Attachment browser
Files attached to notes can be seen within the notes, but if you want to browse all the attachments of all notes, click this toolbar button. It gives an overview of attachments

View attachments
Attachments can be clicked. This one is a video clip and clicking it plays the video in a window. Clicking a document would open it in its associated app, such as Pages or Numbers

Photos and videos
Click the last button in the first set of toolbar buttons to open this panel. It enables you to browse your photos and videos and drag and drop them into new or existing notes

Notes Test out the latest options

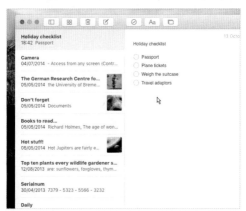

01: Add a checklist

When creating a note, click the checklist button (circle and tick) in the toolbar. Press Enter for a new item or press it twice to end the checklist.

02: Use the checklist

A checklist is very easy to use – you just click in the circle next to each item. It is coloured in and a tick is drawn. Clear an item by clicking the yellow tick icon.

03: Add files

Drag files from the desktop or a Finder window to add them. Photos display in full, but some items shows a filename, such as the Word file shown here.

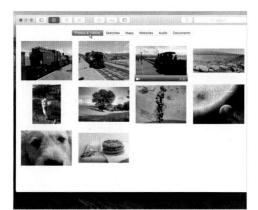

04: View attachments

Click the second button in the toolbar to view attachments that have been added. They are organised into categories, so click the top tabs.

05: Use Quick Look

Quick Look can be used to view attachments. Right-click one and select Quick Look or click one to select it and then press the spacebar. Press Esc to close.

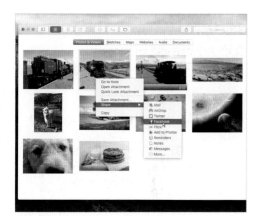

06: Share attachments

Want to share an attachment like a photo in a note? Just right-click an item and use the Share menu. You could share a photo on Facebook, for example.

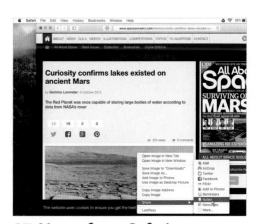

07: Notes from Safari

Notes is part of the sharing facilities in many apps, like Safari. Click the Share button in the toolbar or right-click an item on the web page.

08: Create web notes

The selected item or the page can be stored in a new note or it can be added to an existing one in the Choose Note menu. Click Save when done.

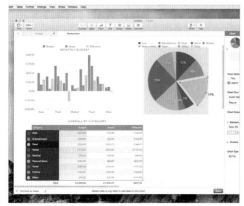

09: Save maps

There are many ways to create notes using Share in apps and here is one. Using the Maps app, click the Share button and select Notes to save this.

Keep your contacts in an address book

Get to grips with the Contacts address book and master its iOS-like layout

Often overlooked, the Contacts app (previously known as Address Book) is an important element of OS X. While it might not be the first thing you open in your dock, it's the hub for all your contacts and makes sure that apps like Mail run a lot more smoothly. It seems only fair, then, that the address book has been given an El Capitan overhaul, too. It now sports a cleaner, simpler interface that before. It is easy to create and edit contacts and you can also share them

effortlessly. Managing your database is easy too as the app can sniff out duplicates and merge them with existing contacts in a single click. You can also create Smart Groups by entering what criteria to include and omit. Read on to find out more.

"An overlooked but important element"

Contacts Explore your address book directory

01: A whole new look

The first thing you'll notice about the app is that its view is very similar to that of its counterpart in iOS. It's looking a lot cleaner, for one thing.

02: Find a friend

Searching is as simple as typing a name straight into the search box. Results are displayed in real time and Contacts will highlight any matches.

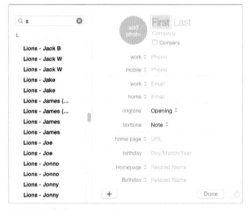

03: Add an entry

Click on the '+' icon under your contacts to add a new one. You can change what the default template includes in Contacts' preferences.

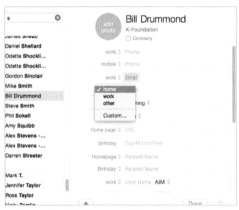

04: Business and pleasure

Contact details can be categorised by type, such as work or home. Click on the type next to the detail and select one from the list to change it.

05: All a Twitter

You can add new fields, such as Twitter usernames, to this version of Contacts. Clicking on a Twitter username will take you to the Twitter app.

06: Share the details

Click on the Share button underneath a contact card to email that contact to somebody else. Contact cards will be attached in vCard format.

Navigate your contacts

Find your way around the address book's interface

iOS-like interface

In keeping with El Capitan's move to be more like iOS, Contacts sports a new interface that is very similar to the one found on the iPad or iPhone. And like iOS, it's clean, simple and textured

Getting social

Contacts includes contact detail fields such as Twitter, Facebook and Skype usernames, allowing you to easily integrate social media details into your list of contacts for quick access. They are even compatible with the native Mac apps

Create new contacts

Clicking on the '+' button at the bottom of the interface will allow you to create a new contact card into which you can enter all manner of details. As you will discover, building up a database rammed with contacts is incredibly easy

Sharing is simple

The Share button makes it even quicker to send contacts. It's fully integrated with Mail and certainly saves a few mouse clicks when it comes to sharing your details

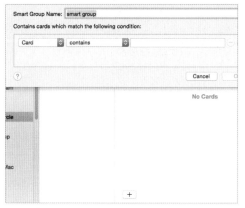

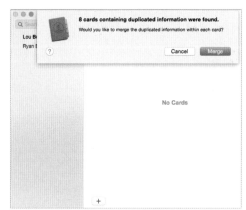

07: Get a group

Clicking on the View menu will bring up the option to Show/Hide Groups. Activate it to bring up a side column with all of your groups listed.

08: Smarter grouping

Smart Groups allow automatic grouping of contacts by certain details. Click 'New Smart Group…' from the File menu to set one up.

09: Look for duplicates

Click on the Card menu and choose the Look for Duplicates option to source multiple cards and merge/delete them from your database.

Build documents with Pages

Whether you need to create a letter, CV, work report, poster or newsletter, Pages is perfect for the job

At first sight, Pages looks just like a word processor and it's true that it can create simple letters and documents. However, there is a lot more to this application, as it can create visually exciting publications such as flyers, posters, newsletters, brochures and much more. The app has been designed to make the task as easy as possible,

and this edition has some great features. For example, there are some fantastic templates to get you started, as very often creating a publication is just a matter of selecting a template and replacing the text and images with your own. It's brilliantly simple. Other new features in this latest version include interactive charts, sharing facilities on iCloud and a whole lot more.

"This edition has some great features"

Pages Create publications from templates

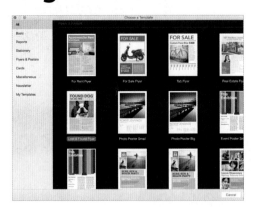

01: Select a template
When Pages is started, click the New Document button to open the template browser. When Pages is open, just select File>New, then pick a template.

02: Edit the text
The template contains text and images, but it's easily replaced. Double-click on the heading, for example, and type in a new one.

03: Replace the images
Click the picture icon in the corner or Ctrl-click a photo to replace it with one from your iPhoto library, iCloud or photo stream.

04: Format the text
When text is selected, the panel on the right provides all the formatting options you need, such as font selection, alignment and so on.

05: Layout options
Select the Layout tab in the panel on the right to access features such as multiple columns to give the text a newspaper or magazine look.

06: Expand sections
Many options are hidden, so click the triangle next to each section heading to expand it. Expand Spacing, for example, for line spacing options.

Master the Pages interface
Tools and features for document design

Sharing options
You can share links to the file on iCloud where it can be accessed with a web browser. Alternatively the file can be sent via Mail, Messages or AirDrop. This makes accessing it far simpler

The toolbar
The toolbar lists all the items you can insert into a document, such as shapes, photos, music and movies, charts and tables. Hidden comments can be added too, for help during the design process

iCLOUD SHARING
These document files can be created on your Mac's disk drive, but there are advantages to storing them in iCloud. For instance, this makes your files available on all your Macs and iOS devices, so you can begin a document on the Mac and continue on the iPad and vice versa. Pages documents shared on iCloud can be accessed by anyone you give the URL to, which means you can get instant feedback.

Interactive charts
Interactive data charts can also be placed in your documents. The buttons that are displayed next to them enable you to step through different data values and instantly see the changes in action

Style and layout
The Style and Layout tabs automatically change depending on the text or object that's currently selected. This whole panel is replaced with new options when working with charts and photos

07: Add shapes
Click the Shapes icon in the toolbar to add lines, arrows, curves and predefined shapes. Click the dots at the bottom to view the items.

08: Shapes and text
Add a shape, such as a speech bubble, drag it into position on the page, click inside it and you can easily enter some text.

09: Share it
Click the Share button in the toolbar to access the sharing options. The document can be put on iCloud and links shared on Facebook and Twitter.

Create and save a custom template

Save your best ideas permanently within Apple's word processing app

 One of the reasons many people will use Pages as their primary app for creating documents is the vast selection of templates that can be used. The templates are a great way of getting a starting point of what you want your document to look like, before you go ahead and add your own twists. However, on occasion it's not uncommon to be unable to find a template that really suits your needs, but thankfully Pages still has you covered. Users are able to create their own custom template, save it and then use it whenever they see fit. Plus if you're really proud of it, then Pages also has a share feature where you can distribute your new template to friends and family. Here's how to go about it.

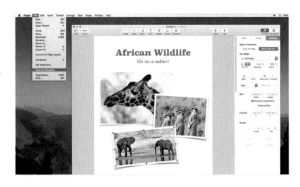

"Pages also has a handy share feature"

Pages Design your own template

01: Start from scratch
Open the template chooser in the Pages app and select the Blank template at the top of the window. This is the blank canvas for a custom template.

02: Add basic text
Select the Text tool from the toolbar and add text elements to your template in the boxes provided. You can make it as brief or as convoluted as you like.

03: Format text
Use the Format menu to bold, italicise and alter the colour of all the text. You can also use this menu to change the sizing and spacing.

04: Import images from Photos
Open the Media tab from the toolbar and select Photos. Highlight a photo to import and press the Insert option on the bottom right of the window.

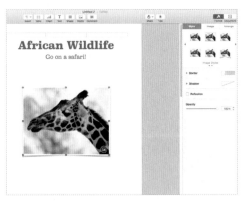

05: Alter image style
Now use the side menu to alter the components of your image. Formatted images are a great placeholder for any future images you import.

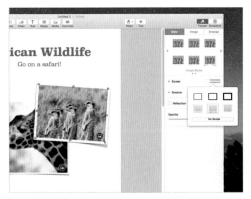

06: Add extra elements
Add the further elements of your template, via the toolbar. You could add secondary images, or perhaps a new table, chart or other form of media.

Manage custom templates
Permanently save your custom template creations

Delete a template
Right-click on any template and select the Delete option if you're looking to cut down on your library of templates. Be warned, there's no way to recover a deleted template, so use this option wisely

Edit names
To make your custom templates more recognisable, double-click the default name to edit them. When you then click off the name, you should find it automatically saves

BORROWING ELEMENTS
One of the best ways to make your own template is to borrow the best elements from Pages' other default templates. A simply copy and paste on the elements you like can help you put together the perfect custom template without having to design it all from scratch. Don't worry though; you can still save it as an original custom template!

My Templates
When you load up the Template Chooser, you'll find the various different options listed down the left of the window. Select the My Templates option at the bottom to find all of your creations

Choose to share
You're able to send your custom templates to various contacts by using the Share option that sits on the toolbar within Pages. There's a plethora of different sharing platforms to choose from

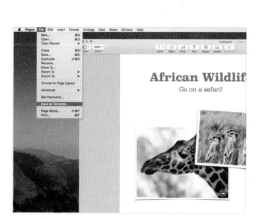

07: Save as Template
Open the File tab before selecting the Save as Template option at the bottom of the menu, when the custom template is done. Wait for it to save.

08: Give it a name
Double-click on the name of your custom template to change it (in the My Template section). Back out of the menu to permanently save it once you're finished.

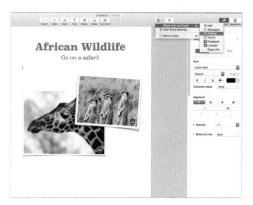

09: Share your template
Use the Share option at the top of the menu to send custom templates to contacts. For a quick solution, use AirDrop to send it to nearby devices.

Create a spreadsheet in Numbers

Ensure your data is well presented and calculates perfectly with the excellent spreadsheet features of Numbers

Spreadsheets may scare you, and with good reason – they are not always easy to use. Microsoft Excel is a very powerful spreadsheet program, but it's complex. So is Numbers, but it delivers all of the functions you need in the simplest way possible and it even offers up explanations to help you out. With a range of templates and the ability to add tables,

resize them, calculate and choose from a range of maths options, you will soon be populating your tables with reams of data.

You aren't confined to one sheet either, as you can edit multiple ones at once by selecting the Sheet button in the toolbar. Numbers makes it easy to work with each one, providing you with a tabbed options pane.

"It delivers all of the functions you need"

Numbers Get to grips with spreadsheets

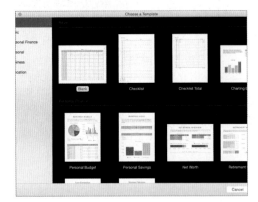

01: Choose a template
First choose from a selection of useful, presentable templates. They are sorted by categories including Business, Personal Finance and Education.

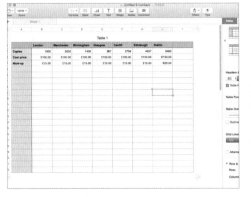

02: Input data
We've selected the Basic template. Spreadsheets have rows, columns and cells, so click each cell to add data. You can use words and numbers.

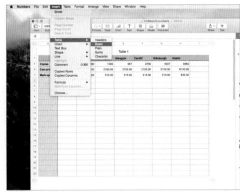

03: Add new tables
As well as using the table in front of you, try adding more via the Insert>Table navigation. Table types are shown in the right-hand box.

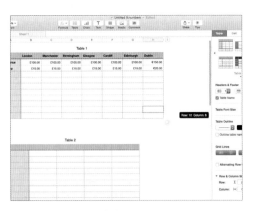

04: Resize tables
By using the arrow icon in the bottom-right-hand corner of a table, you can resize it. Refer to the row and column numbers for guidance.

05: Alter the colours
Now choose cells to colour. Click the Cell tab, click Fill and select Alternative. To change alternate row colours, click Alternating Row Colour under Table.

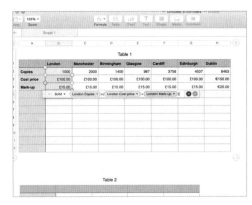

06: Add formulas
Click a cell where you want a total to be displayed. For a simple sum, type '=SUM'. You'll need to define cells to work with.

Find your way around Numbers

Make presentable spreadsheets within minutes

The tabs
This window lets you view the options available for the overall table, cells, text and the arrangement of the spreadsheet. Try clicking on each one to discover what editing options it offers

Title
Tap the word Untitled-Edited at the top of the screen and input a new name that best describes the project or spread you'll be working on. You can save this to the iCloud and to your Mac

HIGHLIGHT CELLS

When creating a formula for your spreadsheet, you don't have to type in the table co-ordinate (such as B2, C9 and so on). You can simply start off the formula (ie =SUM) and then click on the cell that you want to form part of the formula, similar to Microsoft Excel. This is very helpful for speeding up the process of calculations and eliminates any potential errors.

The table
A table is made up of rows and columns and can be a combination of words and text. You can change the table make-up in the Options window to suit whatever kind of table you're looking to create

Add functions
If you want to add a particular function, a table, a chart and more, then just use the toolbar icons at the top of the screen for easy access. This makes creating and adjusting your tables much simpler

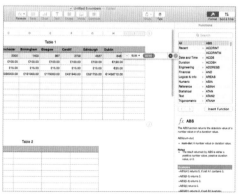

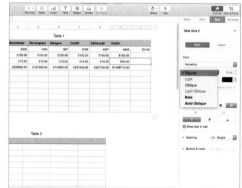

07: Produce the sum

To multiply the final two boxes by our first, type =SUM(B2x(B3+B4). Copying and pasting this cell speeds the task for the remaining calculations.

08: Calculate rows

You can also calculate rows. Available functions appear in the right-hand panel and each of them is categorised and explained in full.

09: Change text

Of course, spreadsheets aren't just about numbers. You can control the size, font, wrapping and style of text under the Text tab in the right-hand panel.

Learn to visualise data in Numbers

Turn mundane data into something special
with the help of charts and graphs

One of the best things about Numbers is that it's a great place to manage all your data in a single area without having to use any third-party alternatives from the Mac App Store. Although having pages of data may be beneficial to you, it can be difficult to read and differentiate between when not labelled appropriately. However, Numbers includes some fantastic chart and graphical options that help add a visual aspect to your data.

Each chart you choose to use to represent inputted data can be heavily customised to suit your specific tastes or the data it's based on. Use the following steps to learn how to completely visualise from top to bottom and create the perfect accompanying charts.

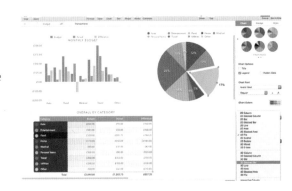

"Numbers includes some fantastic chart and graphical options"

Understand your options

Numbers includes various
features to explore…

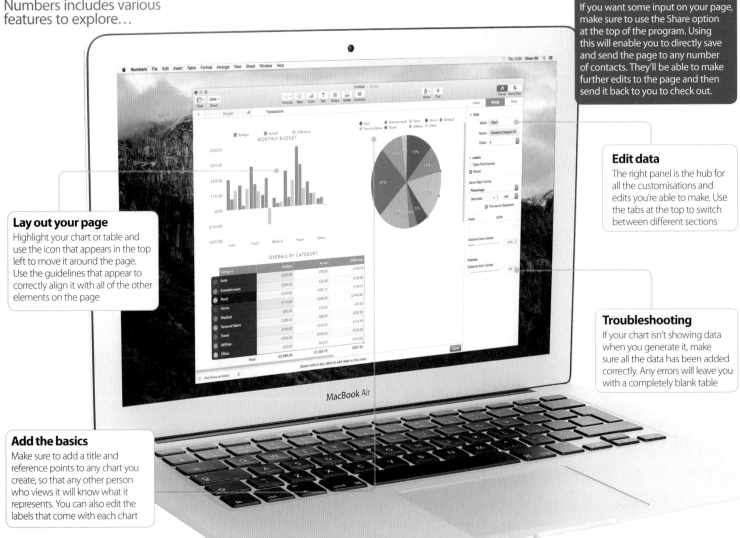

SHARE WITH FRIENDS
If you want some input on your page, make sure to use the Share option at the top of the program. Using this will enable you to directly save and send the page to any number of contacts. They'll be able to make further edits to the page and then send it back to you to check out.

Edit data
The right panel is the hub for all the customisations and edits you're able to make. Use the tabs at the top to switch between different sections

Lay out your page
Highlight your chart or table and use the icon that appears in the top left to move it around the page. Use the guidelines that appear to correctly align it with all of the other elements on the page

Troubleshooting
If your chart isn't showing data when you generate it, make sure all the data has been added correctly. Any errors will leave you with a completely blank table

Add the basics
Make sure to add a title and reference points to any chart you create, so that any other person who views it will know what it represents. You can also edit the labels that come with each chart

Numbers Create charts in Numbers

01: Input data

Create a table of data in Numbers. Apply various colours and stylise the table using the toolbar located on the top of the program, if necessary.

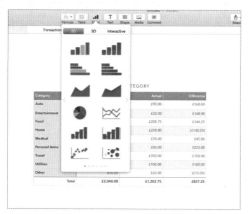

02: Select a chart

Highlight all the data and select the Chart option from the top of the menu. By default, you'll be able to see the array of 2D charts that are available to use.

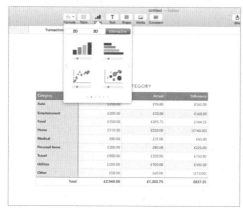

03: Interactive charts

Select the Interactive option if you want to use a chart that can be heavily edited and is generally more appealing to look at.

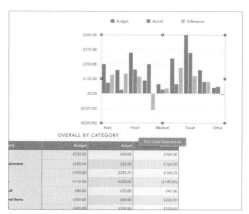

04: Edit data

After selecting the chart you want to use, your data will be applied to it on the page. Select it and press Edit Data References to begin adding changes.

05: Background and borders

The right side panel will now be filled with customisation options. Use the drop-down menus to add a background or add a border.

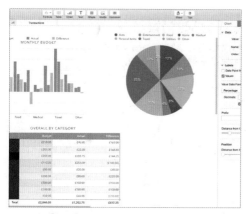

06: Edit data

Double-click on a specific part to edit data. A new Data section will appear on the right side of the app for you make further edits.

07: Move data

Select the Distance from Center option to move a portion of data away. This is a good choice if you want to highlight a specific section in a pie chart.

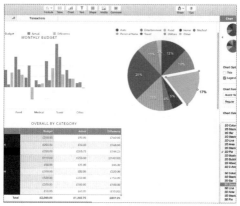

08: Change charts

To change how your data is displayed, highlight the chart and select the Chart Type option to convert it into a completely different chart altogether.

09: Final edits and arrange

Make final edits and line them up on the page. Guidelines will appear, letting you know when each one has been lined with the other items.

Keep notes to help you present

Create presenter notes for you to refer to
when showing off your Keynotes

Keynote makes it simple to create fantastic presentations, thanks to its easy-to-use but surprisingly powerful tools. Whether you want to create a simple text-based presentation or you need something a little more creative, with images, videos and animations, Keynote gives you all the tools you could possibly need, all with just a couple of clicks. But once you've created your presentation,

Keynote doesn't just stop helping you. When you stand up in front of a group of people and give your presentation, it can still help you.

You can use the Notes tool to write down important points that will display on your Mac's screen, so only you see them. It not only makes presenting easier, it will also make you look incredibly professional, and preparing your notes doesn't take long at all.

"Keynote gives you all the tools you need"

Presentation screen explained

Understanding how to use
Keynote's presentation tools

Builds remaining
You can see the number of builds remaining on each slide above the right-hand box. This will only appear if you have applied animations to your slides before hitting Play

Close the presenter
If you want to exit the presenter at any time you can click the 'x' button in the top-right corner of the screen, or simply press Escape to go back to your normal Keynote window

Coloured bars
The bars at the top of the screen denote the status of your presentation. Green means you are ready to progress to the next slide or animation with a click, while red means it's in the middle of an animation

Next slide
On the left is the screen that your viewers can currently see displayed on the external display, while the right-hand box shows what is coming up next, either in terms of animations or slides

KEYBOARD SHORTCUTS
When you use this view to work with your presentation, you can use a number of keyboard shortcuts to make your life easier. For example, with a single keystroke you can pause your presentation and turn the screen white or black, or skip back and forth through individual builds or whole slides. To see the full list of commands, click the '?' icon in the top-right.

Keynote Add presentation notes

01: Open Notes

Open the Notes viewer. Open a Keynote and choose View>Show Presenter Notes to bring up the Notes section at the bottom of your window.

02: Add a note

To add a note, click in the new bar and type it in. The Notes section will remain at the bottom of the window even when you switch between slides.

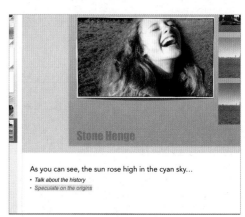

03: Format notes

Click on the Format button and you'll have options for customising your notes. You can change fonts and colours, and add bullets if necessary.

04: Start rehearsals

Once you've finished your notes, you can start rehearsing your presentation. Choose the Play option and select Rehearse Slideshow.

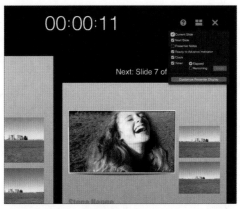

05: Customise your screen

To customise your view, click this icon in the top-right and choose the options that you want to appear on-screen while you present.

06: See your notes

Make sure the Notes section is ticked and you'll see that your slides move to make room at the bottom of the screen for the notes you previously wrote.

07: Edit your notes

Change the size of the notes in your Rehearsal view by clicking the bigger or smaller letters in the top-left of the Notes bar, or click Edit to make changes.

08: View your slides

If you want to see an overview of all your slides, click the Show Navigator button in the top-left and type in the slide number in the top box.

09: Play your slideshow

When you're ready to present, connect your Mac up to an external display or projector and hit Play to start with your notes appearing on your screen.

50
Essential
Mac Apps

The ultimate guide to the Mac apps you simply have to have

Finding and installing Mac apps is easier than ever, thanks to Apple's brilliant Mac App Store. It works by letting you install apps with just a click, and you can be assured that they will be safe for the Mac device you are using. You can still download and install apps from anywhere on the web, but the App Store is by far the most efficient and safe way to add new software to your setup. The apps extend the functionality of any Mac greatly, and without them your choices are limited as to what you can do. There are thousands available, and they cover near enough every conceivable subject or task that you need to complete. This feature will highlight the essential apps from every app category, and hopefully narrow down your search for the best of the best. Your choice of apps is genuinely unlimited.

Essential apps

5 essential apps

The Lost Watch 3D

Price: £1.49/$1.99 **Developer:** Igor Panichev

Not all wallpapers are the same, and The Lost Watch 3D proves that. Besides looking beautiful, it will show you the current date and time, and also lets you personalise it in a rather creative way. It can work as a wallpaper or a screensaver, and there are multiple themes to choose from. If you want to add a personal touch, then simply choose a photo, and it will be shown inside the pendant displaying the time. However, an app like this isn't about the features, but how good it looks and how well it works, and it succeeds in both areas.

Go for Netflix

Price: £2.99/$3.99
Developer: FIPLAB Ltd

This app is a great solution for heavy Netflix subscribers – mainly because it enables you to access your account without loading up a web browser. This way you get quick and easy access to Netflix's huge collection of TV programmes and movies. Go for Netflix isn't an official app, but it is well designed and features hotkey and gesture support. Check out the awesome Auto-Pause/Resume feature too.

Eat The Fish 2016

Price: £1.49/$1.99 **Developer:** Tuyen Mai

How this, a game, can find itself in the Entertainment section as opposed to, say the Games section shows that the App Store isn't impeccably organised. However, as a light distraction it is well worth a look. The aim is to consume as many small fish as possible while not getting chomped on by the bigger fish yourself and you're competing against others for top spot.

MPlayerX

Price: £1.49/$1.99 **Developer:** Zongyao Qu

MPlayerX is an upgrade to your Mac's built-in QuickTime Player. By default your Mac is programmed to play a select amount of files, but MPlayerX brings compatibility for virtually any file type you can throw ar it. A perfect app for anyone with a big movie collection on a NAS drive or external hard drive.

Shazam

Price: Free **Developer:** Shazam Entertainment

Shazam has been around for quite a while and it is a brilliant little app that will ensure that any music your Mac hears will be instantly identified. Handy if you're listening to the radio while working and you missed the name of the band or artist currently playing. So good that it's been incorporated into mobile technology.

Entertainment
Have a whole lot of fun on your Mac

The word 'entertainment' can cover a multitude of things. From listening to internet radio to watching movie clips and enjoying clever screensavers, you can entertain yourself in almost any way you like. It is a broad category, and is hard to define completely, but it is also a category with a wealth of apps that will help you pass your spare time. You can learn magic tricks, watch Earth from space, or simply sit back and watch a realistic fireplace fill your Mac screen. The days of computers being used purely for business are over; now, you can use them for any activity you like. Entertainment is one activity that everyone should spend some time enjoying on their Mac – the only dilemma is choosing from the huge range of apps that are designed to make everyday life a little more fun.

■ The presentation of The Lost Watch 3D is stunning

■ Media is recreated perfectly in MPlayerX

■ The Shazam app is just as good now as it's always been

> "There are a wealth of apps to help you pass your spare time"

■ Have some light fun with Eat The Fish 2016

■ Neon Drive will give you a stunning trip down memory lane

Games
Have fun and keep your brain engaged

Gaming has historically been somewhat lacklustre on the Mac platform, but the huge growth of iOS gaming has transferred to its bigger brother. Popular titles in the puzzle and strategy categories have long been standard, but there are now many hundreds more options available, most of which are at very cheap prices. To complement these simple titles, there is now a variety of high-end arcade titles available, some of which actually rival games consoles in terms of quality, longevity and addictiveness. You can choose almost any game type you like, depending on your preferences and the budget available, and can be sure that the games you like to play are available. Every possible genre is covered, and once you start you may find that you play games on your Mac more than anything else. Everyone needs some fun from time to time, and a Mac is the perfect tool to help you relax and enjoy yourself.

■ The sinister themes and characters of the series are taken to the heavens in BioShock Infinite

5 essential apps

Unmechanical

Price: £7.99/$9.99
Developer: MP Digital

Mechanical is a mind-boggling puzzle adventure that is guaranteed to put your brain to the test. It is easy to pick up and play, but Mechanical gets very tricky towards its conclusion. It combines puzzle solving (more than 30 to be precise), deep exploration and an engrossing atmosphere as you work hard to taste freedom. In total, there's over three hours of gameplay.

Leo's Fortune

Price: £4.99/$6.99
Developer: 1337 & Senri LLC

Originally an Apple Design Award winner on iOS, Leo's Fortune has now been ported over to Mac with some brilliant results. Voyage through stunning environments, dodging traps and solving puzzles on your mission to follow the trail of gold. The aim is to uncover the truth behind Leo's stolen fortune, and it's so addictive you won't stop until you find everything out.

Never Alone

Price: £10.99/$14.99
Developer: MP Digial, LLC

This atmospheric game combines elements of platform and puzzle and is based on a traditional story of a boy and his dog's search for the source of an eternal blizzard. You can guide both characaters in single player mode or team up with a friend and solve the various puzzles co-operatively. Striking to the eye and fiendish in puzzle, it's a beautifully produced game that lives long in the memory.

Neon Drive

Price: £7.99/$9.99
Developer: Fraoula

If you're a fan of retro arcade games and pulsating 80s synth music, then you've probably just comes across your new favourite game. It's inspired by that classic era of gaming, which at its heart is a beautiful-looking, futuristic, obstacle-dodging thrash-around. For such a small outlay you get seven levels to complete, packed with multiple twists and turns to ensure hours of enjoyment.

BioShock Infinite

Price: £22.99/$29.99
Developer: Aspyr Media

This epic first-person shooter takes all of the captivating characters, sinister events and stylish visuals that we have grown to love about the series and places them in the sky – the flying city of Columbia, to be precise. The high-tempo action is aided by the introduction of Sky-Lines, a network of metal struts that you can latch onto to traverse the cloud city quickly (and score impressive kills to boot).

Essential apps

5 essential apps

Kindle

Price: Free **Developer:** AMZN Mobile LLC

While your new Mac comes with iBooks as standard, you may already be familiar with the Kindle service. You might have a Kindle or Amazon account and have bought books on it. Well, if so, Kindle has a presence on Mac in the shape of this app. A great reading experience on the bigger screen, the Kindle app syncs with all other devices and gives you access to over one million books in the Kindle Store, including classic bestsellers and new releases.

Any.do

Price: Free **Developer:** Any.DO

Over 15 million people use Any.do, the simple and powerful to-do list app, to stay organised every day – and it's easy to see why. For a start, it syncs between all your devices, so you're always up to date. Any.do will give you handy reminders, and enables collaboration between multiple users. You can even attach notes and files to your to-dos.

Vinoteka

Price: £25.99/$34.99

Developer: Elodie Morin-Rager

Serious devotees of wine like the thought of having their own wine cellar and, whether you have one or not, you can now experience this feeling through Vinoteka. It will let you monitor every aspect of your wine collection, and is particularly useful for businesses involved in this industry. No matter what your level of expertise or interest, this app is a true example of what can be achieved on a Mac.

Yummysoup!

Price: £10.99/$14.99

Developer: Kenneth Humbard

Yummysoup! has been created to let you bring all of your favourite recipes to one place. You can import recipes from your favourite sites or add text notes that your friends have given you. The presentation is professional, and really does help to bring the recipes to life.

iLove Undelete

Price: £3.99/$4.99

Developer: Wu Yang

Ever accidentally deleted a file from your Mac? Well, trying to get it back is a very long-winded process, and one that needs some expert knowledge. Step forward, iLove Undelete, the new app that will restore deleted files, as long as you haven't restarted your Mac.

■ Vinoteka's presentation is about as good as any app gets

Lifestyle

Tailor your Mac to fit in with your life

We all have different lifestyles, hobbies and interests, and as such a wide range of apps are required to cater for the majority. This particular category is more wide-ranging than any other because it covers all of our interests. From waking up in the morning to keeping a diary, all of these and more can fit in the Lifestyle category. With the right choice of apps, and used properly, they can be truly beneficial to your day-to-day life, and it is worth checking as many as possible to ensure that you are using the ones that are right for you. It is testament to the creativity of Mac developers that even the most obscure of interests are covered by Mac apps, and it goes to show just how flexible and powerful the platform truly is. Whatever your lifestyle, there will be an app for it.

■ Effortlessly restore files you've accidentally deleted

■ Recipes come to life in Yummysoup!

> "The right choice of apps can benefit your day-to-day life"

■ The Kindle app makes reading on Mac a breeze

■ Discover new SoundCloud mixes with SoundMate

■ Remix tracks on the fly with VirtualDJ

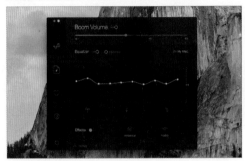

■ Boom 2 will liven up your Mac's speakers

■ Djay's authentic turntables make you feel like a real DJ

Music
Get down to the sound of the beat

The days of playing instruments and recording the resulting sounds to make music could be numbered. You can now create music in thousands of different ways, and record your output in extremely high quality. People now have the capacity to use instruments that haven't been designed yet, and have fun searching for new music using apps that understand their tastes. No matter what you want to do in the musical field, you can now do it, and some of the solutions also suit professional musicians. Songwriters, guitar players and producers can all use complex apps to create new work. DJs can mix music, and individuals can create completely original ringtones. Music has truly reached the digital age, and the digital age has brought music to anyone, no matter how talented they are. Now, we can all create music, just as we wanted to do when we were children.

5 essential apps

Logic Pro X

Price: £149.99/$199.99 **Developer:** iTunes S.a.r.l.

 Logic Pro X is a complete set of creative tools for any musician who wants to write, record, edit and mix music. It comes with a huge collection of instruments, effects and loops, making it easy to get crisp and authentic sounding accompaniments on your tracks. Novices can get up and running quickly thanks to production-ready templates, while one-step track setup and a single-window interface allows you to work fast with easy access to all of the tools you need. With 40 built-in instruments, 80 different effects and over 1,700 samples, this is a studio boffin's nirvana.

VirtualDJ Home

Price: Free

Developer: Atomic Productions America

 There are some apps that you can pick up for free from the Mac App Store that really make a mockery of some paid-for apps. VirtualDJ Home is a great example of this. It's used by some of the biggest DJs in the world to mix songs, and features a cutting-edge beatlock engine to ensure your tracks stay on the beat. Even bedroom DJs will be creating perfect remixes here.

Boom 2

Price: £10.99/$14.99

Developer: Global Delight Technologies

 It's no secret that the sound that comes from your Mac's speaker isn't very good. It's pretty tinny, actually. The audiophiles among you will want to download Boom 2, which enhances and optimises the sound of music files to instantly transform your listening experience.

djay Pro

Price: £39.99/$49.99

Developer: algoriddim GmbH

 If you've ever wanted to be a DJ, but didn't have the confidence to try it, you now can with this brilliant app. The feature set is immense and the presentation is realistic, so you have no excuse to not play around with your music and spin some virtual discs. You can even 'scratch' them like a true pro.

SoundMate for SoundCloud

Price: £3.99/$4.99 **Developer:** Deng Gao

 SoundMate for SoundCloud is a social network for musicians and music lovers, populated by big-name acts showcasing their latest projects and aspiring musicians who upload their own tracks to get feedback. The community is friendly and it is a great place to share sounds with other users.

5 essential apps

Reeder 3

Price: £7.99/$9.99 **Developer:** Silvio Rizzi

When it comes to news aggregation services, few are as popular as Reeder. If you want a clean, smooth and easy to use news reader, then you'll want to grab a copy of Reeder 3. Put simply, it's the best at what it does, providing you with a home for all the news you could possibly wish to read. Reeder has support for multiple services, including Instapaper, Feedly and NewsBlur. Thankfully, the design of the app takes heavy cues from El Capitan – even the font is the same system one used across OS X and iOS.

NewsRack

Price: $7.99 (US only) **Developer:** Ole Zorn

NewsRack takes the middle ground between news readers that attempt to offer lots of clever effects and the more simple RSS readers. It strikes the balance well, and brings a speedy experience which is particularly useful if you follow many different sources. With integration to third party services like Instapaper, you may find this app to be the perfect one for satisfying your news gathering needs.

Downcast

Price: £5.99/$7.99

Developer: Jamawkinaw Enterprises

Not everyone wants to get their news by reading it digitally. A great alternative is to listen to podcasts, and Downcast is an ideal deal way to manage and listen to a library of your favourite podcasts. Downcast first made its name on iPhone, but has been nicely ported to Mac. It's packed with features, but at its core it is a place to search, subscribe and download audio. It fully supports iCloud syncing too.

Pocket

Price: Free **Developer:** Read It Later, Inc

Pocket provides a handy service for storing all of the web articles and videos that you don't have time to explore presently in the cloud and makes them accessible through any device. You can even read articles offline, making this idea for those long commutes.

Pulp

Price: £7.99/$9.99 **Developer:** Acrylic Software

This innovative news reader transforms your favourite news sites into your own personalised newspaper, making scanning through the news quicker and more enjoyable than ever before. By putting multiple news feeds onto a single page, Pulp lets you quickly browse through headlines to find hot topics.

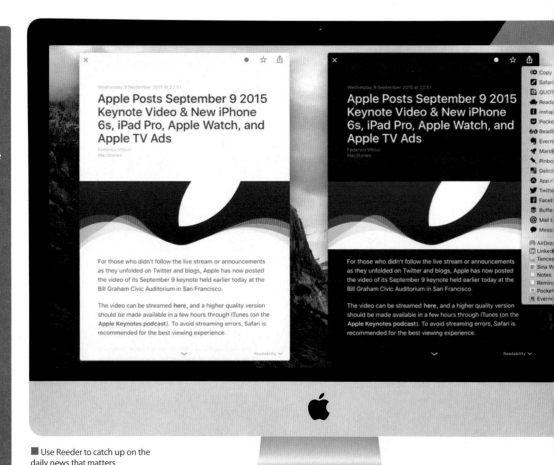

■ Use Reeder to catch up on the daily news that matters

News

Keep informed on everything in the world today

It used to be that the best way to keep up with the news was to visit websites. Of course, this works well for sites like the BBC, but for specialist topics it can involve hunting around for the right places. Some Mac apps are now capable of recreating news provided by websites in a way that is more friendly, logical and easier to read. Other apps will automatically grab the latest news and present it on the desktop, and the options for reading a variety of topics are almost unlimited. No matter what the topic or your visual preference, there will be a solution that suits the way you want to catch up with the world around you. Indeed, some are so good that you may never visit a traditional website for news again.

"Some Mac apps are capable of recreating news from websites"

■ Whole articles can be read without leaving the NewsRack app

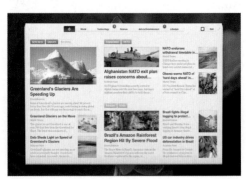

■ Get your news feeds in your own personalised newspaper with Pulp

■ The PicFrame app can make even dull photos look stunning

■ Use Macphun's Filters for Photos to add filters to your editing suite

■ Get the power of Photoshop for a fraction of the price with Affinity Photo

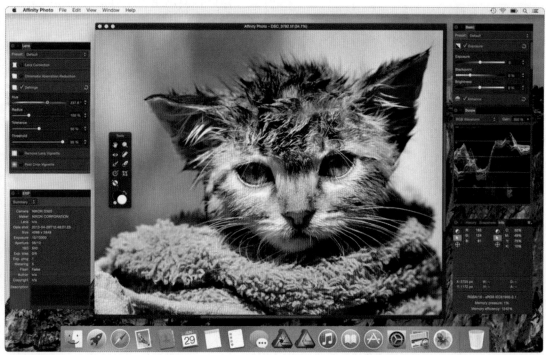

Photography

Store your memories, and create new ones

Photographers will tell you that, often, a lot of the work required to create a great photograph happens on a computer after the photo has been taken, and this makes the Mac platform ideal for anyone with an interest in this field. It doesn't matter if you are experienced or new to the world of photography because there will be a solution, and the majority are designed to be as easy to use as possible.

From adding speech bubbles to making photos look like they were taken many decades ago, you can do almost anything you want with a Mac and a collection of digital images. You can take this as far as you like or just play around, but either way, the platform and available apps will offer you everything you need to get started and enjoy the world of photography for professional or personal reasons.

■ Pixlr gives you everything you need to tweak images to perfection

5 essential apps

Affinity Photo

Price: £39.99/$49.99
Developer: Serif

The old saying goes you need Photoshop to do some real powerful image editing on Max. Affinity Photo proves you don't, giving you the power of Photoshop at a fraction of the price. It's engineered for professionals, and includes supports for unlimited layers and retouching effects of the highest standard. Affinity Photo is so good, Apple made it one of their apps of the year.

Filters for Photos

Price: Free
Developer: Macphun

Filters for Photos does exactly what its name suggest, supplying you with endless filters to add to your built-in Photos app in OS X. Accessible as a third-party extension, this wonderful free app gives you creative filters to transform your images. Apply one of the filters, tweak the strength of it and then save it to your Photos library or share it via all the usual social sites for the world to see.

PicFrame

Price: £0.79/$0.99
Developer: Active Development

A good frame can make even the dullest pictures look attractive, and this affordable app features 67 adjustable frames, with support for up to nine photos in a single frame. Once you have composed your photo arrangements, you can share them on Facebook or Twitter, or just enjoy gazing at them on your desktop. For the price, this is a brilliant app for showing off your snaps.

Autodesk Pixlr

Price: Free
Developer: Autodesk

Autodesk is more famous for creating super-powerful 3D rendering software for Mac than free image editors, but Pixlr displays all the trademarks of Autodesk's brilliant apps. Pixlr is a great way of transforming everyday images into works of art. Whether you're applying a quick fix or adding effects, overlays and borders, Pixlr has everything you could possibly need – and it's free!

Flume for Instagram

Price: Free
Developer: Rafif Yalda

Viewing your Instagram account online is a pretty unwieldy way of using the photography social network, but Flume for Instagram solves that problem with its gorgeous edge-to-edge imagery, direct messaging and upload support. Flume lets you view images and videos at full resolution in their original aspect ratio. A must-have for Instagramers.

Essential apps

Fantastical 2 will keep your calendar in
perfect shape and keep you productive

Productivity

Maximise your output

Productivity takes many forms, and there are solutions that will help you be more productive, no matter what your need or speciality. Everything from creating text documents to building databases can fall into this category,

and it is without doubt one of the more diverse categories, encompassing a wide range of apps. If there is any task that you need to be more productive at, there will likely be a solution available. It may require some careful searching, but a solution will arrive that could potentially speed up every aspect of your work, which can have major benefits for almost everything you do with your desktop or laptop. Sometimes, the smallest solutions offer as many benefits as the larger apps and you should take time to see if a collection of smaller apps will work better than one large app.

"There are many great productivity solutions"

■ Scrivener's distraction-free mode is brilliant

■ Multiple views are available in Evernote

■ Capture your thoughts and create to-do lists with Wunderlist

---

5 essential apps

Scrivener

Price: £34.99/$44.99

Developer: Literature & Latte Ltd

 If you're a professional writer, or writing is a daily hobby for you, Mac users don't have a huge selection of choice. Scrivener is, according to best-selling novelist Michael Marshall Smith, "the biggest software advance for writers since the word processor." Scrivener is multi-purpose, so it acts as a typewriter, an organiser and a journal. Scrivener works so well because the focus is entirely on your words.

Fantastical 2

Price: £39.99/$49.99

Developer: Flexibits

 The best third-party apps are the ones that hugely improve your everyday Mac experience. Fantastical, for example, adds a huge amount of features to your stock Calendar app. You can add events quickly, integrate additional calendars from third-party sources and link with your contacts.

1Password

Price: £49.99/$64.99

Developer: Agilebits Inc

 If you want to apply extra security to your Mac and protect all of your various user names and passwords then this app works directly with your browser, saves all of your details and then effortlessly creates strong, unique passwords for each site. The app can then automatically and securely log you in, enter credit card information and fill in registration forms, all while encrypting your info with one password.

Wunderlist

Price: Free

Developer: 6 Wunderkinder GmbH

 If you need an outlet for all of your creative ideas, or you just need an efficient and robust app for creating quick and easy to-do lists then this app fits the bill perfectly. Through a simple interface you can get down your notes and share them with others.

Evernote

Price: Free **Developer:** Evernote

 Evernote is a hugely popular online note system and can help you manage and organise many aspects of your life. This free app brings all of your notes and quick synchronisation to any Mac and is designed to offer all of the main features on your desktop all of the time. If you like to store thoughts, images and notes then this is essential.

5 essential apps

Twitter

Price: Free **Developer:** Twitter, Inc

Amazingly, it is only recently that Mac users have had the option to switch from using Twitter through a web browser to an actual app, but the good news is that this free download is easy to use, comes with a smart interface and has been well worth the wait. Through Twitter, you can follow your interests and get instant updates from your friends, industry experts, celebrities and see what's happening around the world. You can do everything through this app that you could through the website.

Tweetbot

Price: £7.99/$9.99
Developer: Tapbots

While the official Twitter app is more than serviceable it is low on killer features. Of the third-party options available to you, Tweetbot is the one we'd recommend. It's designed specifically for Mac (so it looks great and works with Notification Center) and features support for multiple accounts – a must for anyone who balances work and personal accounts. You can view everything with multiple columns or windows too.

App for Instagram

Price: Free
Developer: Joacim Stahl

Ever been frustrated by there not being a standalone app for Instagram? Well there's a quick and handy solution in the Mac App Store in the form of Joacim Stahl's App for Instagram app – a discreet widget-like app that lives in your Mac's main menubar and gives you direct access to your Instagram feed. All you do is tap the camera icon in the menu bar and your feed drops down, from where you can like and comment on any post just like the mobile app.

Pin for Pinterest

Price: Free
Developer: Chatsworth and Whitton Limited

This app takes your Pinterest addiction to a whole new level by allowing you to instantly browse your Pinterest account without having to open your web browser. You will need Pin Pro to upload new images, but this app at least allows you to fuel your Pinterest interest.

FaceTime

Price: £0.79/$0.99 **Developer:** Apple

Just because you run an older operating system on your Mac doesn't mean you have to miss out on cool apps like FaceTime. You can grab a Snow Leopard-optimised version of the app from the App Store and video message anyone in your Contacts app.

Social Networking
Stay connected with a variety of fantastic apps

Social networking has grown to be one of the most used forms of internet communication, and for some people the big services like Twitter and Facebook take up the majority of their online time. Each service has websites associated with it, but rarely is the web experience as good as standalone apps on a desktop or mobile. There are apps available that can sit on the desktop and update you as they work, and others that offer more features than the social networks do officially. Other solutions attempt to bring all of your social networks together in one place, and even allow you to update multiple sites at once. If you use any of the social networks, then there are apps available that will completely transform the way that you communicate with friends and strangers. It's just a question of finding the ones that work best with the way that you like to talk.

> "Transform the way that you communicate with friends and strangers"

■ Video message friends and family with FaceTime

■ Tweetbot uses a column view to ensure you can balance multiple accounts

■ Tap the App for Instagram icon and your feed drops down

Essential apps

5 essential apps

Swing It Pro
Price: £109.99/$149.99
Developer: FKE Datakonsult AB

Golf is all about the swing. Without a good technique, your scores will be higher and your enjoyment less. You can either pay lots of money to get some coaching, or purchase this app and learn at home. It uses videos to help you visualise what you need to do. You can crop the videos, create notes and work in your spare time. It isn't cheap, but compared to professional coaching, it could produce similar results, and ultimately save you money.

Simplified! Yoga
Price: £4.99/$6.99 **Developer:** Tony Walsh

You don't need us to tell you that yoga is a great way to get – and stay – fit. If you're keen to learn what it's all about, and you respond well to video tuition, Simplified! Yoga will be a great addition to your Mac. The app gives you 211 videos to watch (this actually makes it really good value for money), and searching is easily done, as is rating your favourites. You can even see your video watching history as a handy way to keep track of your progress.

iPlayBook
Price: £1.49/$1.99
Developer: Aletheia Management Partners

This useful app enables a basketball coach to use their Mac as a tactical drawing board. With no complicated menus to navigate, you can be up and drawing in no time. Arrange players' positions easily according to your strategy and even draw special moves with your mouse, then share it with the players or staff.

Sports Feed – Live Scores Widget
Price: Free **Developer:** SportsFeed LLC

Any American sports fans will want to get their hands on this app. It lives in your Mac's Notification Centre and lets you instantly see live scores of your favourite team's latest match. You can personalise your widget with NFL, NBA, MBL teams and much more.

Yahoo Sports
Price: Free **Developer:** Yahoo! Inc

This is another widget that lives in your Mac's Notification Centre, providing you with up-to-date scores, fixtures and stats to all your favourite teams. All the American sport you can think of is covered, but also top international soccer leagues from all over the world. A great addition if you want at-a-glance information and don't want to load up a browser.

■ With Swing It Pro you can analyse any aspect of the perfect golf swing

Sports
Make the most of your sporting abilities

Sports is a category that is broad in that it has to cater for a wide range of different activities. Within each sport there are further groups of people; coaches, players, fans and so on. This means that app developers have to build a variety of solutions for every conceivable activity, and this category alone highlights just how popular the Mac platform is for apps. No matter what sport you enjoy, you should be able to find an app that will increase your enjoyment or participation. From getting up-to-the-minute timings on motor racing laps to building strategies and plans for a team you coach, you can do it with a Mac. As a fan, you can also find specialist apps that will present news and gossip for particular sports, and this includes information from official sources, which are presented in a unique way for the desktop.

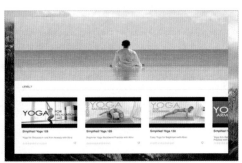

■ Use your Mac as a way of learning a new sport like yoga

■ Check your favourite team's score in Notification Centre

"No matter the sport, you should be able to find an app to help"

■ Map out your basketball team's tactics on your Mac

■ iStopMotion feels like creating a home video

■ Save your custom settings in Compressor and they'll
appear in Final Cut Pro X too

Video

Watch the latest and best videos in high-quality output

The world of digital video is a curiosity in that most people will have already been exposed to it, but few of the creators will take the time to enhance their media. It is very much seen as a static media form; you take a video and leave it as it is to view at a later date. However, you can do so much with your creations, and there are all sorts of apps to help you manipulate all of your personal and work-related videos. You can add special effects, funny commentary and even incorporate them into professional presentations. The beauty of the Mac is that even the lower-end systems are able to cope with memory-intensive video production really well. The platform is designed to cope with all types of media, even high-definition video files, and the video apps available on the Mac App Store make it all work together in an even more efficient manner.

■ Final Cut Pro X is powerful enough to use 3D titles

5 essential apps

Final Cut Pro X
Price: £199.99/$299.99
Developer: Apple

When it comes to editing video on your Mac, there is no better choice than Final Cut Pro X. It's an app used by real Hollywood directors to store and manage their footage, apply pro-level effects and share it with the waiting world in all sorts of formats. Final Cut can help you get smooth audio too, as well as tweaking the colour in your clips. There's even green screen features to try out.

Motion
Price: £39.99/$49.99
Developer: Apple

Motion is another app made by Apple, and another must-have for video editors. Motion lets you customise Final Cut titles, transitions and effects. You can mess around with 2D or 3D titles, and apply a variety of effects with the help of over 230 behaviours. It's a brilliant way to get natural-looking motion without any programming knowledge. The app's 64-bit architecture supports layered effects.

Compressor
Price: £39.99/$49.99
Developer: Apple

Compressor is an app that anyone using Final Cut for professional reasons will want to download. It adds power and flexibility to Final Cut's export process, customising output settings, helping you to work faster with distributed encoding and giving users access to a comprehensive set of delivery features. Compressors work flawlessly, even if you throw batches of video at it.

iStopMotion 3
Price: £39.99/$49.99
Developer: Boinx Software Ltd

Stop motion is a video effect that most people had no access to… until iStopMotion came along, that is. With this app, you can spend time creating a stunning stop-motion films, where inanimate objects can be made to move, which will surprise anyone that you show it to. The time required to become adept at using this is surprisingly low for the potential results.

Smart Converter
Price: Free
Developer: Systemic Pty

If all you require is a simple and effective video converter app then this free offering ticks all of the right boxes by being able to handle hundreds of different file types to enable that they play on all of your favourite devices. All you have to do is drag and drop a media file into the app and then choose a conversion type. It will only convert what is needed, making it one of the fastest of its type around.

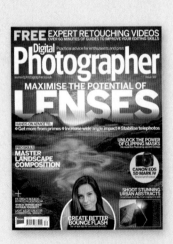

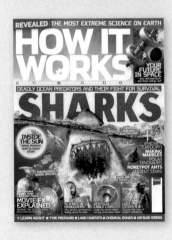
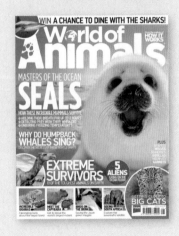

SAVE UP TO **40%** ON THE NEWSSTAND PRICE

Never miss an issue

13 issues a year, and as a subscriber you'll be sure to get every single one

Delivered to your home

Free delivery of every issue, direct to your doorstep

Get the biggest savings

Get your favourite magazine for less by ordering direct

TRY 3 ISSUES FOR £5

HOW TO USE

EVERYTHING YOU NEED TO KNOW ABOUT ACCESSING YOUR NEW DIGITAL REPOSITORY

To access FileSilo, please visit http://www.filesilo.co.uk/bks-B51

01 Follow the on-screen instructions to create an account with our secure FileSilo system, or log in and unlock the issue by answering a simple question about the edition you've just read. You can access the content for free with each edition released.

02 Once you have logged in, you are free to explore the wealth of content made available for free on FileSilo, from great video tutorials and online guides to superb downloadable resources. And the more bookazines you purchase, the more your instantly accessible collection of digital content will grow.

03 You can access FileSilo on any desktop, tablet or smartphone device using any popular browser (such as Safari, Firefox or Google Chrome). However, we recommend that you use a desktop to download content, as you may not be able to download files to your phone or tablet.

04 If you have any problems with accessing content on FileSilo, or with the registration process, take a look at the FAQs online or email **filesilohelp@ imagine-publishing.co.uk**.

Apple Music Basics

Learn the basics of starting with Apple Music. With Apple's streaming music...

OS X icon pack

78 redesigned OS X icons inspired by iOS's new flat design. Made...

Using iCloud Photo Sharing

iCloud Photo Sharing is a quick and easy way to share photos...

NEED HELP WITH THE TUTORIALS?

Having trouble with any of the techniques in this issue's tutorials? Don't know how to make the best use of your free resources? Want to have your work critiqued by those in the know? Then why not visit the Bookazines or iCreate Magazine Facebook page for all your questions, concerns and qualms. There is a friendly community of experts to help you out, as well as regular posts and updates from the bookazine team. Like us today and start chatting!

facebook.com/ImagineBookazines
facebook.com/iCreateBookazine